GUS:
A Nun's Story

GUS:
A Nun's Story

Patricia Nolan Savas

BRIDGE PUBLISHING, INC.
S. Plainfield, N.J.

Unless otherwise indicated all Scripture
has been quoted from the *New American
Standard Version* of the Bible.

Gus: A Nun's Story
ISBN 0-88270-648-9
Library of Congress Catalog Card # 93-71482
Copyright © 1993 by Patricia Nolan Savas

Published by:
Bridge Publishing Inc.
2500 Hamilton Blvd.
South Plainfield, NJ 07080

To my devoted husband, Peter,
who, for almost twenty-five years,
has patiently held my balloons.

*That I may know Him, and the power of His
resurrection and the fellowship of His sufferings,
being conformed to His death; in order that I may
attain to the resurrection from the dead.*
(Phil. 3:10,11)

No Scar?

Hast thou no scar?
No hidden scar on foot, or side, or hand?
I hear thee sung as mighty in the land,
I hear them hail thy bright, ascendant star,
Hast thou no scar?
Hast thou no wound?
Yet I was wounded by the archers, spent,
Leaned Me against a tree to die; and rent
By ravening beasts that compassed Me, I swooned:
Hast thou no wound?
No wound? No scar?
Yet, as the Master shall the servant be,
And pierced are the feet that follow Me;
But thine are whole; can he have followed far
Who has nor wound nor scar?*

— *Amy Carmichael*

*From Toward Jerusalem by Amy Carmichael, p. 85.
Published by Christian Literature Crusade, Fort Washington, P.A.
Reprinted by permission.

Contents

Foreword

Little words can carry a large message, especially when they are spoken by the Lord. And this is what Jesus said:

It is the Spirit who gives life; the flesh profits nothing; the words that I have spoken to you are spirit and are life. (John 6:63)

In short, the words of the Lord are vital to our spiritual well-being. However, for those words to take on form and flesh, that which is spiritual and vital must become structural and verbal — something we can touch and feel and hear. The incarnation of God's Son is our example: He took on our humanity that the clear truth of our Father's holy love could reach us through a language we could understand — the language of life.

Through Jesus, the Father drew near to us — and drew us near to Him. Through the structure of a human body and the sound of human words God personally ministered His life and His love to all who would hear and respond. And many did; and in so doing they found a new destiny and dignity in the royal family of God.

Our Father's desire for a warm, loving family relationship has never changed. He still desires to reach out to a lost and wayward world with His redeeming love. But how is this to be achieved? This is where we come into the picture. As Spirit-born members of Christ's Body here on earth, we are the living Church in action — visible, tangible expressions of His life. We are the only form of Jesus that others can see, hear, and touch, individually and corporately. But what do they see? What do they hear? What do they touch?

Sadly, church structure and language, so essential in our day for the "Word to become flesh," can slowly be severed from their spiritual source and significance. Apart from God's Spirit, ecclesiastical programs, doctrine, and ritual can become ends in themselves and be reproduced in a religious form which is lifeless, loveless, and powerless. As history has shown, it is a danger which every Christian tradition and denomination faces, no matter how sincere or orthodox they may be.

The Scriptures plainly declare that there is no substitute for a personal relationship with the Lord. But only the Holy Spirit can make His presence live in our hearts. He alone can enable us to turn from our lifeless forms of religion to the reality of a relationship with God. Through His gifts and graces, the Holy Spirit again desires to bring the fresh breath of God into the Church of His beloved Son. And it is happening — life by life, person by person — in every tradition that is willing to follow the path to a new Pentecost for our time.

But where and how? Where is it to be found — this redeeming road from "religion to relationship" — and how can it be pursued? In *Gus: A Nun's Story*, Pat Savas, as Sister Augusta, describes her discovery and personal journey along that road with honesty, humility, and above all, charity. While her story is from the perspective of her religious heritage, many of us will find numerous matching thoughts and feelings in our own pursuit for an intimate relationship with God. Readers will discover, as I did, that beyond the interest which a fascinating and well-written life story always generates, there will be another response. It is the strong, sympathetic beat of our hearts as God's Spirit draws us onward along that same road of spiritual revelation.

Pat Savas is a professional educator, counselor, and writer. But more than that, she is a modern-day prophetess with the sensitive heart of a poet. It is a rich deposit from which to draw, for it allows her to describe her search for spiritual reality with both personal feeling and divine insight.

As we follow her footsteps along the road from religion to relationship, our hearts will be filled with faith and anticipation. Through her story, we shall see how the guiding hand of God will wisely, lovingly, persistently, and patiently draw to Himself every life that earnestly seeks to know Him in Spirit and in truth. Though our paths may be paved with many faults and failures — our own and those of others — the Lord will sanctify and direct each step until we find ourselves at home in His embrace.

The word-pictures which Pat paints of her journey honestly reveal the dark colors of pain and disappointment carelessly brushed by family, friends, and even religious leaders to whom she turned for help, healing, and affirmation. But nothing is ever wasted when we learn to look only to the Lord — and for the Lord — during the stormy seasons of our lives. It is during such times that God delights in encouraging and directing us with unexpected rainbows of promise; and there are many such radiant scenes splashed throughout this remarkable story. You cannot miss them!

It is the destination — the road's end — that really counts. Be ready for a revelation of God's love that can change your life, just as it did for your author. Open your heart to Pat's life message, for she is speaking from her heart, and that of our dear Lord. For those whose lives are empty, lonely, and strangely sad, take courage; for this is a true story that ends with a happy beginning. Read with hope and expectation; you will not be disappointed!

Robert C. Frost
August, 1992
Escondido, California

Preface

We are assured that Jesus Christ will one day return for His Church, whom He compares to a wife "having no spot or wrinkle" (Eph. 5:27). Yet, as we behold her pathetic state today, we wonder if He'll even recognize her. She has been severely battered by denominational disputes, hierarchical politics, religious dogmatism, and so many other problems. Shepherds who were entrusted with her care have forsaken her in their own pursuit of gold and glory.

Although this book chronicles the pilgrimage of a former Roman Catholic nun from the sterile entrapments of religion to a vital, joyful relationship with God, the message extends to those of every denomination who are longing for an authentic, life-giving relationship with the Savior, but are being given the emptiness of religion instead. One only has to witness the pervasive disillusionment within many congregations to know that the church in America is now faced with the resulting tragedy.

My compassion runs so deep for the victims of spiritual abuse and abandonment that for a long time I could not find words to adequately express it. One evening while I was watching a news broadcast, a scene was dramatically imprinted upon my mind which seemed to express my heartache and concern.

In a famine-ravaged land, a mother who was obviously dead was lying on the ground as an infant was trying to nurse from her withered breast. Unable to obtain nourishment, he would alternately wail pitifully, then try to awaken her with his tiny fists. A Red Cross worker reached out to him but the bewildered child clung desperately to the corpse, shrieking in terror at the thought of separation. After all, was not this his mother—the one who was supposed to feed him, care for him, protect him from harm?

As you ponder this image in your heart, I leave you with the hope and prayer that you will benefit from my journey and discoveries.

Patricia Nolan Savas
February, 1993

Acknowledgments

I am grateful to:

All the people who faithfully prayed that this book would be published.

Mary Froese, who typed the original manuscript simply because "That's what the Lord wanted me to do."

Sherwood "Woody" Wirt and the San Diego County Christian Writers' Guild, for their unfailing encouragement.

Jay Dove, who helped me overcome my technophobia by introducing me to the computer in a non-threatening way.

Diana Blanc, my dear friend and prayer partner, who has stuck "closer than a brother" (Prov. 18:24).

Introduction

This is a true story. Several persons mentioned in this book, including my own parents, are now deceased. To prevent embarrassment, I have changed the names of almost all of the nuns.

Strictly speaking, the nuns of the order to which I belonged were not really nuns at all. "Nun" is a term that applies to cloistered communities of women who remain in their convents, devoting their lives to prayer and contemplation.

The community of Sisters of Charity was founded in the seventeenth century by St. Vincent de Paul in France with the express purpose of getting the female religious out of the convent to work in the world among the poor. For that reason, he used such terms as "sisters" or "daughters," and avoided those things typical of the cloistered life. In this biography, for the sake of convenience and clarity, I have employed the most commonly used religious terms.

Although it was painful for me to relive many of these experiences as I was writing this book, I can honestly say that I have no bitterness in my heart, nor do I seek sympathy from anyone. My heavenly Father, whose will is holy and perfect, chose to bring me along this uncommon path for His glory and for my perfection, to form me into the image of His Son Jesus, the Messiah. I would not have wanted it to be any other way.

Several years ago I suddenly awoke one midnight for no apparent reason. Usually when I cannot sleep, I read the Bible or pray; sometimes I just sit in the stillness and listen. This particular evening, however, I had a strong urge to turn on the television set.

I came across a secular program in which an interviewer was conducting a discussion with three former Roman Catholic nuns and three ex-priests. In the course of the interview, they all discussed the how's and why's of their leaving the religious life and what professional decisions they had made after their respective departures. All of them had gone into psychology, psychiatry, counseling, social work or related fields.

As the program progressed, an inexplicable sadness permeated my spirit as I realized that not one of them had mentioned any sort of relationship with Jesus Christ or anything even remotely connected to their former religious ideals. Toward the end of the program the interviewer finally asked, "Are any of you still searching for God? Have all of you given up the quest?"

Only one man answered, "No, I haven't given up. I'm still looking for Him. I hope to find Him someday."

Instinctively, I found myself reaching out my hand toward the television set and saying, "Don't give up."

Essentially, that is what this book is about:

Don't give up.

Note: The term "Messiah," a synonym for Christ, is used throughout this book to remind the reader of the Jewish roots of our Christian faith.

1

A Hole In My Soul

Hear, O Lord, when I cry with my voice,
And be gracious to me and answer me.
When Thou didst say, Seek My face, my heart
said to Thee,
Thy face, O Lord, I shall seek.
Do not hide Thy face from me,
Do not turn Thy servant away in anger;
Thou has been my help;
Do not abandon me nor forsake me,
O God of my salvation!
For my father and mother have forsaken me,
But the Lord will take me up. (Ps.27:7-10)

Mark called as soon as he got my letter. "I'll be there to see you off."

"No, please don't do that. It's hard enough for me to leave my grandmother. Seeing you there would make it doubly difficult."

5

For a few seconds there was total silence, then he said, "I love you. I'll wait for you."

With a knot constricting my throat, I whispered, "Don't wait more than a year. If I'm not back by then, I've decided to stay. You must make a new life for yourself."

I hung up the hallway phone and quickly walked back to my room, hoping that none of the other girls had overheard the conversation. (There was no such thing as a private conversation in this women's dormitory — Roble Hall.)

Sitting at my desk, I just stared at my history book. "How will I ever make it through these exams? I can't concentrate on anything right now. What does it matter, anyway? Ten days from now, my life will be over!"

Stanford was a fine university but I never really felt I belonged in that secular environment.

Although the campus was scenic and sprawling and the classes were interesting, I sorely missed my all-Catholic surroundings. Pretending to be sophisticated, I never really discussed it with anyone. Who would understand, anyway? The lingering fragrance of the incense after the *Tantum Ergo* at Benediction, the peaceful reassurance of being able to visit the church or chapel at any time, the specialness of daily Mass, the Stations of the Cross during Lent — how I missed them all.

The Catholic chapel—donated by Claire Booth Luce in memory of her daughter who had been killed in a car accident while attending Stanford—was several miles from our residence, as was the Newman Club, the organization for Catholic college students. Since I didn't have a car, it was difficult to attend Mass except on Sundays and holy days of obligation, and even on these days I could go only when I managed to catch a ride.

Coming out of the grueling academic training I had received in Catholic schools, I found the classes at Stanford both enjoyable and easy. At the dinner table one evening I made the mistake of saying, "Compared to what I'm used to, this is a breeze!" The comment was met with immediate silence and icy stares.

Later, Becky, a St. Louis girl whose room was next to mine, grabbed me by the arm and pulled me aside.

"For a bright girl, you have no 'smarts' at all. You never go around making remarks like that. You can *think* it, but don't *say* it."

My naiveté became evermore apparent to the worldly-wise students from the public schools. Becky took me under her wing. One night we were to be studying in her room together. As we carried bags of groceries by the housemother, we cheerfully called out, "Midterm snacks, Mrs. B!" The groceries, in addition to the chips and cookies, also contained a milk carton full of wine. We could hardly contain our giggles.

"Becky," I asked, "did you request a private room when you filled out the application papers?"

"No."

"Neither did I. That's something, isn't it? You and I have the only private rooms on this hall; all the others are double or triple."

"Lor-dy, you are the most naive kid that ever crawled out of convent school ivy. The rest of these gals are WASPs." Seeing that nothing registered, she continued,

7

"You know — white, Anglo-Saxon, Protestant? We, dearie, are the token minorities. You are the 'Cross-back' and I am the Jew!"

"You—mean...?"

"You won't find it written in any catalog, the way they tell you that there are 2.5 men to every woman student, but it's sort of the unwritten code of WASPdom here on 'The Farm.'" The combination of potato chips, pretzels, cheap wine and this stunning news was too much for me.

"I'm getting dizzy — and sort of sick," I moaned.

"Here," said Becky, "lie down on my bed." Placing a damp cloth on my forehead, she continued, "Patty Nolan, don't take it so hard. I've lived with it all my life. You've gotta be tough, you know — have *chutzpah*."

"Sooooo," I groaned, "how do you say that in Gaelic?"

This struck Becky as really funny and she began to laugh uproariously. The mellifluous sound of her laughter was contagious and, even in my weakened state, I couldn't help but join in. Hearing the commotion, the other girls began poking their heads into the room. "What's happening — what's so funny?"

The irony of these WASPs sticking their heads in the door and questioning us about this "inside joke" was just too much. Each new query caused fresh shrieks until I was holding my head, leaning against the wall and Becky was rolling around on the floor, gasping for air. Even girls from the other adjoining halls, hearing the peals of laughter, came to take a look. Soon everyone was congregating outside our door. "What's going on — why are they laughing?"

"We don't know; they won't tell us."

While they were busy wondering, Becky whispered to me, "The mob is forming."

"Yeah," I replied. "This will go down in history — the first cross-burning at Stanford." As the hilarity of the moment again caught us, we grabbed our stomachs and rolled around on the floor — roaring until we cried.

After thirty or so minutes, we were both weak and spent. I finally composed myself enough to head for my room. "Good night, Becky. Thanks for a great time."

"Well, the way I figure it," she said smiling broadly, "you've either got to laugh or cry. I've decided to laugh — glad to see you join me."

You'll never know, my good friend, how many times in the passing years I have remembered your hard-earned optimism. Since that night I've also wondered how many other colleges had such "unwritten codes" before the pendulum swung so far in the opposite direction.

After this revelation, I began to be conscious of my minority status. For the first time, I removed the scapular from my neck. Scapulars were small pieces of cloth — brown or green — worn over the chest and back, attached by strings of the same color. These pieces of material, imprinted with images of Mary and various saints, were supposed to ward off evil and protect us from harm. I did keep my St. Christopher medal on —hanging from a silver chain around my neck. On the reverse side was stamped the all-important message: "I am a Catholic. In case of an accident, notify a priest."

Although my background in the classics was prodigious compared to most of the other students, I was lacking in certain areas of modern literature and philosophy. For the first time, I was exposed to Faulkner, Hemingway, F. Scott Fitzgerald and Henry James, et al. Also, I was faced with the dilemma of being required to read works which the Catholic Church had placed on the Index of forbidden books — such as those of Voltaire, Rousseau, Kant and others.

When I called the chaplain, he responded with what must have been an oft-repeated speech: "You have my permission to read these, always bearing in mind that they are just the ideas of men and often in conflict with Holy Mother Church. If you feel that your faith is being vitiated in anyway, contact me immediately and we'll discuss it."

As I hung up the phone, I thought that it was pointless to even have an Index if people were going to read the books anyway.

Another area that required immediate improvement was my writing. One of the first themes I turned in was returned to me all marked up with comments like, "Technically perfect, but stilted." It had "C" marked on it. I was so dejected I could hardly talk about it. Imagine — a "C"! I showed the paper to Lynne, the only other girl besides Becky that I ever really became close to during my college days. I knew that Lynne was an excellent writer.

One day I had observed her with mild fascination as she pounded away on her typewriter, a cigarette dangling from her lips. "Hey, wait 'til you read this!" she had exclaimed. "This guy wants us to use a first-person, stream of consciousness technique — so, take a look." I remember how amazed I was as I read her daring composition. It precisely described what Lynne thought as she sat in this English teacher's class. She recounted her annoyance at the professor's mannerisms, her boredom and how she escaped mentally by reexperiencing the thrill of riding her horse over verdant hills.

I remember saying to her, "Lynne, you aren't really going to turn this in, are you?"

"I sure am." she said. She did, and she received an "A" on it, with no comments from the professor.

Now, as I showed her my paper, she sighed, "Poor baby, got her first 'C' and fell apart. The trouble with you is that you were taught by those monks so long that you even write like one of them."

Lynne also prided herself on being an agnostic. Anyone who was in any way connected to religion was a "monk" to her. She made no distinction between the pope, archangels, Jewish rabbis, Protestant ministers, Catholic priests or nuns.

"When you write, it's gotta come from here," she exclaimed as she thumped her stomach. "Don't worry about what other people think, or what kind of a grade you're going to get. Just make it honest and real. You admire Shakespeare, don't you? Well, how about what he said: 'To thine own self be true.'"

Lynne taught me more about writing than any teacher I've ever had, before or since.

On Ash Wednesday, the beginning of Lent, I managed to get an early ride to Mass. When I returned with the smudge of gray ashes on my forehead, Lynne exclaimed, "What kind of hocus-pocus is that, anyway?

11

Good grief! You're not going to wear that around all day, are you?"

"It's supposed to be a sign of my penitent spirit."

"You've got to be kidding. Why not paint it red and throw a sari around you, like that girl from India? Then I can do a write-up on you for the campus newspaper, too." Somehow I never minded Lynne's chiding me because she was a sincere friend.

One Sunday morning I overslept. I was really upset because I had to get to Mass before the Gospel was read in order not to commit a mortal sin. Since Lynne was one of the few students I knew on campus who had a car, I banged on her door, "Lynne, wake up! I really need a ride to church!"

Sleepy-eyed, she yawned, "Listen, kiddo, trust me. There is no such place as hell and even if there was, you're too nice a person to go there just because you missed some hocus-pocus one Sunday." Seeing the anxious look on my face, she said, "Okay, just give me a minute." She hurriedly threw on her weekend grubbies — tennis shoes, jeans and an old trench coat. (Lynne dressed like that long before it became fashionable.)

As we got to the church I turned to her and said, "Lynne, you don't have to come in if you don't feel like it, but if you want to, we can sit in the back pew."

"Hmmm," she pondered, and to my surprise she followed me in. During the entire service she sat with her arms folded across her chest. When we got back in the car, she remarked, "Boy — sit, stand, kneel, bow —such gyrations! I figured out why they do it, though — it's to keep you from falling asleep."

I couldn't help but chuckle. "Thanks, Lynne, how about I buy you some pizza?" Pizza had been introduced to the college scene about a year before and quickly had become the rage.

"Listen," she said, "don't tell anyone about this, okay? You'll ruin my good reputation. Of course, I could always say I was at church doing research for a paper on Karl Marx's assertion that religion was the 'opiate of the masses' or something like that." I smiled my response.

While we were eating, Lynne lowered her eyes and posed a question — with a very deliberate casualness. "So, tell me, what do you really get out of this religion stuff?"

As she continued to eat I explained the best way I knew how. I even told her about reading the *Confessions* of St. Augustine when I was fourteen and how often, even in the middle of class, his words would constantly stir me: "Thou has made us for Thyself, O God, and our hearts are restless until they rest in thee."

I told her about my upbringing, the call I felt, my search for God. Other than an occasional "Uh-huh," she just listened.

"Lynne, don't tell anyone else this, but I've wanted to be a nun for a long time — not the kind that's cloistered, but the kind that's out in the world helping the poor. I've pretty much decided to join an order that does that kind of work. I want to be a social worker."

At that point she stopped eating and just sat staring at me as I continued, "The only reason I'm here is to please my parents. They wanted me to try college for a

13

while, but it's just made me more convinced than ever that I want to do something worthwhile with my life. You know, I've seen a lot of totally selfish lives. What will they have to show for it when it's all over? I want to be able to say that my life really counted for something."

"You're right about one thing, kiddo. There are a lot of spoiled brats here and I think it's great that you want to do something worthwhile with your life, but I don't know if it has to be something *that* drastic!" Lynne and I reached a point of mutual acceptance that day.

In bed that night, I couldn't get Lynne's question out of my mind: "So, tell me—what do you really get out of this religion stuff?"

No one had ever asked me that before. It made me think back . . .

* * * * * * * * * *

Because I was basically a very lonely and insecure child, lacking both parental affection and approval, I relished the security which the Catholic religion offered me; my acceptance of the black/white absolutes of the church was complete and unquestioning. We were taught that ours was the only true church because we alone could trace our sacerdotal lineage back to the first Pope and Bishop of Rome, St. Peter. The fundamental teaching of the church was clear and without compromise: "Outside the Roman Catholic Church there is no salvation."

Anyone who was not Catholic was "non-Catholic." The term Protestant was often used to include all those who didn't believe the way we did. No distinction was made with regard to the Orthodox or to various denominations. Jews were not even considered, since they didn't believe in Jesus Christ.

What would be the eternal fate of all those non- Catholics? With the exception of a very few who may have attained what was referred to as "Baptism of Desire," most of them simply would not make it to heaven and would, in fact, end up in hell. Perhaps some extremely holy ones, who would have been Catholic had they known better or been given the chance, would end up in a place called "limbo." This was believed to be a state of rest located somewhere below heaven. Infants who died without the benefit of the Sacrament of Baptism were assigned there. Since they had not attained the age of reason and therefore could not have committed deliberate sin, they couldn't be punished. However, without baptism to wash away the "original sin" they had inherited from Adam, they also could not enter heaven. (That is why Catholics baptize children at such an early age.) In my child's mind, I visualized millions of babies just wafting over green meadows and dangling from puffy clouds, some sprouting tiny wings, whiling away eternity.

By far, that sector of the spirit world which we believed to have the greatest populace was an area of fiery cleansing which, unlike hell, was not eternal. This area was termed "purgatory." (Most of us, in fact, believed that we would go to this fearful place for some duration. We never really had the assurance of having been redeemed by the blood of Jesus, the Messiah). We also believed that by saying rosaries or short aspirations such as "Jesus, Mary, Joseph, have mercy on us," we could collect reprieves called "indulgences" and shorten the sentence of some poor soul burning in purgatory. The hope was that, when he then reached heaven, he would return the favor.

15

Because our minds were considered unreliable instruments for the interpretation of the Bible, the church told us what we were to believe regarding the sacred Scriptures. A minute percentage of Catholic homes may have had one family Bible, usually collecting dust in the living room, but very few were ever read. The priests would read small portions of the Epistles or the Gospel to us during the Mass, and that was the extent of our exposure to the Bible.

The pope was the absolute, final authority in all matters involving faith and morals. When he pronounced something "ex-cathedra" (from the throne) in either of these two areas, it was to be accepted without question. Anyone who believed or acted contrary to these pronouncements was excommunicated — the worst fate that could befall a Catholic. This meant that he could not receive Holy Communion, or go to confession, or participate in the sacramental life of the church.

If a family friend or business associate was getting married or buried, we had to obtain permission from our pastor or bishop to attend the service and we could never participate in the prayers or the ceremony.

My religion was my anchor, the only thing I could absolutely count on in my tenuous existence.

* * * * * * * * * *

"Yes," I pondered, "that 'religion stuff' is everything to me. I'm grateful to be in the only group that is assured a first-class ticket to heaven."

One Saturday, several of us went into San Francisco for theater and dinner. After the show, we were walking in an area outside of Chinatown. One of the girls said to me, "Why don't you go in there and ask to see their menu."

"Well," I responded, "this doesn't look like a restaurant to me. It looks more like a bar."

"No, I think they serve food. Just ask."

Timidly, I went in, searching the room for a maitre d'. As my eyes adjusted to the dark, I noticed couples at the bar and in the dining room. A few of them were dancing. Then gradually I realized that something was very strange. They — were — all — men! The shock propelled me out the door and I stood, aghast, on the sidewalk. I was horrified to the point of speechlessness. The others were laughing hysterically. I had been set up.

During this time at college, Mark and I had exchanged letters and phone calls as he was 500 miles away. He came up for a few dances. I still cared for him a lot, however, my resolve to become a nun was growing stronger.

I had also been corresponding regularly with Sister Bernadette, the Vocation Director of the Sisters of Charity of St. Vincent de Paul who were headquartered in St. Louis. She was a true professional at portraying the life of the sisterhood as a totally fulfilling and exciting dedication to God's poor. If she had been in the secular milieu, she would have made Madison Avenue sit up and take notice.

I knew that entering this order (the only one I was familiar with that included social work in their ministries) would mean leaving my beloved Sisters of St. Joseph of Orange, who were restricted to teaching and nursing. It would also mean leaving my orange groves and my ocean forever, never to return.

As soon as my exams were completed, I returned to Orange. As usual, my parents said very little to me. For once, I welcomed the reticence.

By agreement, everyone told my grandmother that I was going to visit a friend for a few days. When I arrived in St. Louis, I would write and tell her what my plans were. I tried hard to numb myself against the grief of leaving her. I knew that I would never see her again in this life. In those days when you left—it was forever. Seeing my suitcases in the hall, she shook her head, "Look at that girl. She always takes so many clothes for just a few days."

My chest felt like it had a steel band tightening around it. I kissed her on the cheek and said, "Bye, Nama. I'll miss you."

Turning quickly, I jumped into the waiting car so she wouldn't see my tears. On the way to the airport I silently prayed, "Lord, I offer this suffering up for my grandmother, to lessen hers — in this life and in the life to come."

As the plane ascended, I consoled myself with the thought that I was giving my all in the pursuit of what my heroines, the nuns, had told me was the greatest vocation a woman could attain.

Maybe now I would really encounter God as Augustine and Thomas a Kempis and all my revered saints had, and the constant ache in my inner core would cease and the hole in my soul would be filled.

From earliest childhood I had yearned for this completion. How often had I lifted my tiny head to the starry skies, entreating:

"Are you there, God? Do you care? Do you love me?"

2
Out of the World, Into the Frying Pan

Then Peter answered and said to Him,
"Behold, we have left everything and followed
You; what then will there be for us?"
And Jesus said to them, "Truly I say to you,
that you who have followed Me, in the
regeneration when the Son of Man will sit on
His glorious throne, you also shall sit upon
twelve thrones, judging the twelve tribes of
Israel.
"And everyone who has left houses or brothers
or sisters or father or mother or children or
farms for My name's sake, shall receive many
times as much, and shall inherit eternal
life.
"But many who are first will be last; and the
last, first." (Matt. 19:27-30)

19

"We are now passing over the Continental Divide," the pilot announced. This note of geography evoked the remembrance of my fifth grade teacher, Sister Dorothy. The image of her cherubic face made me smile as I gazed out the window at the feathery clouds.

I had taken a bad spill on the asphalt playground. Bending over to help me up, she gently patted me on the arm and said, "All for thee, Jesus. All for thee." She had always told us to unite all of our sufferings with those of the Savior and never complain. "All for thee." How many thousands of times I would utter that ejaculatory prayer during the coming years.

"Are you going to St. Louis for a visit?" the stewardess inquired as she handed me a pillow.

"No — to stay, I think." To stay.

For some reason that infinitive had a peculiar ring to it and it brought to mind my mother's tight-lipped reaction to my leaving. She never said anything directly to me but, turning to a friend who had come to say good-bye, she remarked, "This is just a whim. She's giving up a future and a career for some asinine notion. She'll never stay."

Years later, my sister would observe, "We were her showpieces, you know, but neither of us turned out the way she had planned. You were supposed to be the famous actress or lawyer and I, the doctor. I don't think she ever really forgave us for choosing lives different from the ones she had mapped out for us."

* * * * * * * * * *

My first memories were not of my parents nor my one sibling. When I was an infant, mother placed me with her par-

ents, Michael and Margaret Lowney, and their three bachelor sons, in Massachusetts. My sister lived with my grandmother's sister and her husband, Bridget and William Hogan. Their home was on the other side of town in the affluent area, which my uncles jokingly referred to as "the lace curtains."

For reasons which were never clear to me, my mother and father lived in Rhode Island where they worked.

Grandfather was chair-bound at the time and died shortly thereafter of cirrhosis of the liver and kidney failure. Although he had given up drinking a few years prior to his death, alcoholism still took its final toll.

My mother never attempted to hide the great animosity she held toward him. She often boasted that she was the only one who had ever "stood up to the lout."

Her childhood experiences had seeded deep roots of resentment and loathing within her psyche. Often she admonished us, "Don't ever marry a man you can't control. Only weak women let men dominate them." She included her own mother in that category.

Medicine was really the only love of my mother's life. She had wanted to be a doctor, but finances did not permit it. Also, during that era, there was great prejudice against women becoming physicians. This fact was a source of rancor for my mother throughout her entire life. Often I heard her exclaim, "Some of those doctors are imbeciles. I know so much more than they do."

That may have been true. She was, above all else, the consummate nurse. Brusque and officious in her manner, she demanded maximum effort of all those in her charge, including my sister and me. I don't ever remember having been rewarded or even commended for doing well; it was expected of me. Nothing less than the best was ever acceptable.

Emotional and physical distance was always maintained in our family. I have no remembrance of ever having been held, hugged, rocked or read to.

I once read a biography of Winston Churchill in which the writer delineated the powerful love-hate emotions Churchill had experienced toward his mother. Reared by nannies in the English tradition, he nevertheless longed for the love and approval of his mother, a remote but dominant figure in his life. She was a socially prominent person, renowned for her beauty and intelligence in both British and American societies.

When asked how he envisioned his mother, Churchill described a childhood experience of watching his mother descend the grand staircase of the palace, prepared to greet her many friends and visitors who had gathered in the room below. She was attired in a regal ball gown and bedecked in diamonds. Head held high and smiling aristocratically, she was the remarkable, but for him always unattainable, Jenny Jerome Churchill.

Standing in the snow on the steps of Fairfield State Hospital ,my mother was impeccably dressed in white, from her shoes and stockings to the starched cap on her head. She wore a navy blue wool cape, with one end thrown back to expose the contrasting, bright crimson lining.

The source of both my great admiration and deep heartache, this is the formidable image imprinted on my memory of Alice Lowney Nolan.

* * * * * * * * * *

As I stepped down from the plane in St. Louis, the suffocating effect of the combined humidity and heat left me breathless. This climate would prove to be my great nemesis. As nuns were not allowed air conditioning at that time; it was considered "worldly" — a pampering of the flesh. After I received my full nun's habit, composed of ten pounds of linen and wool, I would often pray for the strength just to be able to function in what seemed like a perpetual steam bath.

"Ah, you must be Miss Nolan," said Sister Mathilde. "Sister Bernadette sent us to meet you. This is Sister Ann."Sister Mathilde nodded toward her cheerful companion as an elderly man picked up my suitcases and loaded them into the station wagon. He drove as the two sisters sat with me in the back.

"Well, we are expecting twenty-six of you postulants in this band (entering group). You are the only Californian. As a matter of fact, you are the only one from any of the western states. All the others are from the midwestern or southern states." Sister Mathilde continued to do most of the talking as we passed through the metropolitan area.

Looking at them, with their starched winged "coronets" and immaculate, large white collars over the blue serge gowns, I wondered how they managed to appear so prim in this sultry weather. "We have over 2500 sisters just in this western province alone, you know. In the eastern province they have almost as many. We are the largest women's order worldwide. It is an enormous responsibility for the Mother General in Paris."

The car began to slow and we turned off the road into a very long private driveway. On either side were large trees in full emerald bloom and hundreds of acres of lawns. As we approached a sprawling Victorian structure, Sister Ann offered, "This is our private hospital, St.

Vincent's." (She did not mention that it was specifically designated for the mentally ill). We continued on the winding road and finally stopped in front of an imposing mansion of the same era and design as the hospital. "This is the Motherhouse."

"Sister Margaret, this is Miss Nolan, from California." Nodding toward me, Sister Ann continued, "Sister Margaret is the Mistress of Postulants, Miss Nolan. You will be completely in her charge during the next nine months. She is responsible to our Lord and to the community for your spiritual formation. You must obey her in all things."

Thus was I introduced to Postulatum, the first stage of my exodus from the world. If, after this initial period, the community decided that I was a suitable candidate, I would be permitted to enter the Novitiate, comprising one year of very severe discipline including total silence. These first nine months, however, were devoted to dusting off the worldliness from our young souls.

Sister Margaret took me to the dormitory where there were rows of alcoves, sections containing one bed and a simple dresser, surrounded by white cotton curtains. Closing the curtains after me, she whispered, "Please remove your clothes and place them on the bed. Put on the articles which are on the chair and when you are finished, come down to the community room to meet the other postulants."

With perspiration dripping from every pore of my body, I exchanged my pink cotton dress for a skirt, blouse, short cape, cap, stockings and plain, laced shoes — all in black. Only the small linen collar attached to the

24

cape was white. "No more wardrobe decisions," I thought. "Basic black — always stylish."

When I walked into the community room, most of the others had already assembled. They were sitting around a long, rectangular table with the Postulant Mistress at the head. "You may each give your name and where you are from. This is all that we will need to know. One of the first lessons you will learn, as you enter religious life, is that we want to leave our former identities completely behind us and never refer to what or who we were before."

As we proceeded with the introductions, eager but anxious voices introduced themselves: "Miss Kelly, Chicago."

"Miss Schmidt, Dallas."

"Miss Donegan, St. Louis."

Twenty-six young women, each searching for what? For God? For fulfillment? For destiny? For a meaningful life in a nonsensical world?

After the introductions we adjourned to the dining room, called the "refectory," for supper. We ate in silence, as one of the sisters read from *The Life of St. Vincent de Paul*.

It is difficult to explain how peculiar this regimen was at first. Sitting on long benches without even acknowledging the presence of those next to us, we would have to nod or motion with our hands to have the butter or salt passed. We had to eat everything which was placed before us, without showing preference or distaste.

I thought that it was strange that they served Cream of Wheat at that evening meal. Watching the others, I followed suit as they placed salt, pepper, butter on the white substance. Swallowing my first spoonful, I thought, "Not the same as I'm accustomed to — with cream and sugar — but okay." Several weeks later I would discover that I had been eating grits.

At the end of each meal an aluminum dishpan and a pitcher filled with hot, soapy water were passed to each one of us in turn. We would wash, then dry our own dishes, roll our flatware up in our napkin, then pass the pitcher and pan to the next postulant. Next to our napkin we also kept a neatly rolled gingham apron which we used for chores.

After supper, the Postulant Mistress called us together and announced, "Usually we have a thirty minute period of recreation at this time, followed by evening prayers. I can see that some of you are weary from traveling, so we will just say 'short prayers' and then go to bed. We always rise at 5:00 a.m., so you'll need your rest tonight. The time after evening prayers until after breakfast the next day is known as the Great Silence. You must not talk at all, except in the case of an emergency. You will have fifteen minutes to get ready for bed. Let us pray."

Standing under the shower, I turned the spigot to cold, half expecting steam to rise from my skin. We were allowed to use the various toilet articles which we brought — but never any cosmetic items; those, like the world we had left behind us, were gone forever.

As my head touched the pillow I thought briefly about my cool Pacific Ocean and grandmother.

* * * * * * * * * *

26

Grandmother took us to Mass regularly and at five years of age, I became aware that we were Catholic. One day, I asked her, "Why can't we take Nancy to church with us?"

"Nancy is Protestant," she replied.

"What does Protestant mean?"

"Her people believe differently about God than we do and, well uh, they killed some of our people in the old country," she replied shortly.

She must have seen the look of horror in my eyes because she immediately added, "No, no — not Nancy, herself. She's a good girl."

I can still vividly recall the aroma of burning beeswax and the flickering flames of the three large votive candles which Grandmother lit every week. They were the twenty-five-cent ones which were supposed to burn for an entire seven days.

One day, I whispered (we always whispered reverently in church where the quietude was all-pervasive), "Nama, why do you always light those three candles?"

In her usual laconic way, she replied, "Those are for your uncles fightin' in the war."

She never said much, but I knew that she was worried about them, so I added my prayer to hers when she gave me a nickel to light a small votive. As the coin clinked down the metal slot, I remember saying to myself, "God, or Mary, or whoever you are, please bring my uncles back."

No matter how far his romps took him, Skippy, my mixed-shepherd pup, would instinctively return at 3:30 in the afternoon to meet me as I stepped off the school bus. Grandmother and he had their tea together. She in her large cup and he in a bowl, both with cream and sugar. In the winter, believing it would ward off colds, she added a half of an aspirin for each of them.

Although considerable reserve always characterized relationships and conversations in our family, at least grandmother was there. She usually wore an apron, with a handkerchief in one pocket and rosary beads in the other. Sometimes I could see her lips move silently and I would ask, "Nama, what are you doing?"

"Sayin' my beads," was her reply.

* * * * * * * * * *

"No," I reminded myself. "You have turned your back on everything and everyone forever in order to seek God. You must never look back. All for Thee, Jesus."

The ringing of the hand-held bell plus a female voice intoning, "Live, Jesus!" awakened me after what seemed like a very brief sleep. We were supposed to answer, "Forever in our hearts," then rise very quickly and kiss the floor. All I could manage was a murmur as my knees thudded on the hard, slick wood. In silence I hurriedly dressed, opened the curtains, tied them around the posts, and went down to the chapel for prayers and morning meditation followed by Mass. This, I mused, was to be the daily routine for every morning of my life.

One of the nuns would read "Point One" of the meditation, followed ten minutes later by "Point Two," then the concluding point. We were all to meditate on the words which were read pertaining to spiritual growth. At the conclusion, the sister in charge (in this case the Mistress of Postulants) would call on someone to briefly share her thoughts on the meditation for that day. This was supposed to make us concentrate on what was read, but most of us had a struggle just staying awake.

If we started to become drowsy, we were supposed to stand up immediately or the sister in charge would nudge us. If we had been thus prodded, we were to rise and remain standing until the sleepiness was conquered. It was not uncommon to see four or five of us, some tottering in various directions, standing during most of any given meditation period.

That first morning I was so entranced with the uniqueness of it all that I managed to stay awake during both meditation and prayers. Gazing around the vaulted Gothic chapel, which was larger than many churches, I thought how wonderfully peaceful it was.

The postulants were placed in the upper right of the chapel, with the professed (full) sisters behind us. On the left knelt the novices. They had entered, two-by-two, hands hidden up their sleeves, eyes always cast down, from the cloistered wing where they were totally cut off from all contact with the community as well as the world for one year. How ethereal they seemed with their white bonnets and shawls — more like the Amish, I thought, than Catholic sisters. Contact with them was extremely rare, but if a postulant or professed sister ever did cross their path, the novice would immediately turn away, head downward, until the other person had passed.

That morning they seemed like a separate species to me. It was difficult to imagine that I would ever be one of them.

* * * * * * * * * *

When I was nine years old, Mother decided to move us to California. My life then became exclusively Catholic. I was placed in Catholic school where I would remain until going to college.

Since my family life was virtually non-existent, I turned to school and religion for fulfillment and recognition. I became the studious, devout ,"good little Catholic girl" upon whom the nuns beamed approval and bestowed honors.

They were excellent educators and strict disciplinarians and they commanded respect. They glided rather than walked; their presence often heralded only by the tinkling of the large rosary beads which hung at their sides. In their neatly starched, white headdresses and black veils ,they gave the appearance of other-worldliness. They seemed to have been born in those "habits" which they wore. Our young Catholic minds never conceived of their having any prior mundane existence, or even regular bodily functions. "Surely," I thought, "this is as close to God and the saints that a woman can ever get on this earth."

* * * * * * * * * *

After breakfast we were assigned to chores — cleaning the kitchen, sweeping the refectory, scrubbing the bathrooms, polishing the dormitory floors, dusting the chapel. Everything was inspected by the Mistress of Postulants. If we failed to complete our assignments according to her standards, we were openly reprimanded and ordered to keep at it until she was satisfied.

Often the professed sisters would pass us and whisper, "This is nothing compared to what's in store for you in the Novitiate." Sometimes they would smile knowingly at each other and mention the "great secret" of the Novitiate. This led to curious speculation on our part during our recreation time. Did they really shave their heads completely at the end of the canonical year? Did they do strange penances? Were there some secret ceremonies never revealed to outsiders?

During the next nine months we would be taught how to walk, talk and deport ourselves. "Miss Ryan," the Postulant Mistress would admonish, "We have no antelopes in this community. Go back up those stairs one at a time, in lady-like fashion!" or, "Miss Pedretti, it is contrary to modesty to saunter along like that, swinging your hips. Now, cross your arms under your cape, take small steps and walk down that hallway." (So they weren't born with that glide, after all.) If anyone's voice became too loud during recreation, the Postulant Mistress would ring the bell next to her place at the community room table and warn, "You must speak in moderated tones at all times. It simply is not befitting someone in the religious life to be boisterous."

We would also be introduced to "the Rule," which governed every area of our lives, twenty-four hours a day. These precepts, which every founder of a religious order had to submit to Rome for approval, were read to us constantly during instructional periods and during meals sometimes, until they saturated our very existence.

We were told that we must practice "custody of the eyes" at all times; we were never to gaze around curiously, nor to look a person of the opposite sex directly in the eyes. "The sisters shall keep their eyes cast modestly down at all times." We were never to touch another person, male or female. "They shall avoid all physical contact, even with their own sisters." We received incessant warnings about avoiding "particular friendships," which we were told could lead to serious violations of the vow of chastity. Every time I heard this mentioned, all I could think of was that bar in San Francisco and that thought sent shivers down my spine.

To prevent such intimacy, we took our recreational periods in threes instead of twos. If any two persons were observed getting too close, they were put on notice. We were to treat everyone equally and never reveal our innermost selves to anyone except our superiors or the priest in the confessional. Surrounded by people, we were nevertheless virtually alone.

On the fifth day after my arrival, I went to see the Mistress of Postulants to ask permission to write to my grandmother. As was the custom I knelt before her chair, kissed the floor and waited for her to speak first. After I explained the circumstances, she told me to sit down.

"Here in Postulatum, we are a little more lenient with regard to writing or receiving letters. When you get to the Novitiate, all of your incoming mail will be censored and you will be permitted to write one monthly letter to your parents which will be read by the Novice Mistress. However, I think you should write to your grandmother now. Remember to be cheerful and edifying. No matter what we are going through in our own lives, we must always keep up the appearance of smiling courage and never let the others know of our crosses. Remember that feelings don't count — you will hear that again and again in this community — make it a dominant axiom in your life. Sanctity lies in the *will*, not in the emotions; we simply must not pay any attention to our feelings.

"If there is nothing else, you may go now. Oh, by the way, Miss Nolan, when you walk with your head held up like that it gives the appearance of haughtiness. Try to lower your chin a little, in a more humble demeanor."

"Yes, mother, thank you," and I kissed the floor again.

Walking away from the mistress' office, I could hear my high school drama teacher's voice: "When you stand out on that stage, you must take command of it. Hold your head up, stand very erect, project your voice to the opposite wall until it comes back to you. This is what we call 'stage presence.' You'll never be a truly great actress without it."

* * * * * * * * * *

Gwenn Holly Simpson was a laywoman and a professional, an associate of the Pasadena Playhouse. She expected the highest standards of us. In our freshman year we presented the medieval morality play, Everyman, and J. M. Synges' intense drama, Riders to the Sea. Under Mrs. Simpson's direction, I played Hamlet's Ophelia and then won second place in the Southern California Shakespeare Festival with a portrayal of Desdemona in Othello.

In my junior year she encouraged me to portray Eliza Dolittle in Pygmalian, for which I was given the gold medal at the University of Southern California's speech and drama competition.

Although she never actually said so, I think Mrs. Simpson recognized the veiled pathos of my life and, through her devotion and encouragement, provided me with an acceptable vehicle of expression — the stage.

Sorry, Stage Presence, you'll have to take your final curtain call now. Exit, stage left.

3

An Exceedingly Narrow Way

Enter by the narrow gate; for the gate
is wide, and the way is broad that leads
to destruction, and many are those who
enter by it.
For the gate is small, and the way is
narrow that leads to life, and few are
those who find it.

(Matt. 7:13,14)

"Dear Folks,

Well, I've been here four months now. It certainly seems like I've truly entered another world.

"I can't tell you how grateful I was for the first northern breeze that came exactly on the second day of September. I was kneeling in the chapel early in the morning when I felt the crispness brush my cheek. I kept saying, 'Thank you, God.' It meant that the dreadful summer heat was nearly over. They keep telling us that we must die to self in all areas and I'm really trying to do that, but apparently I'm far from it as yet.

"There have been some humorous incidents involving the weather too. About a week after I arrived, we had our first summer storm. The initial shock of lightning and thunder was so frightening that instinctively placing my hands over my ears, I dove for cover. The other girls just laughed and said, 'You'll get used to it.' I guess, having lived in California for so many years, I had forgotten what thunderstorms were like. It brought to mind how I would hide in the closet as a youngster until grandmother had sprinkled the entire house with holy water while she explained that it was only the good angels fighting against the bad ones.

"One day, soon after my arrival here, I discovered one very last blossom on a lilac bush which someone had planted near the kitchen. Captivated with the remembrance of that delightful fragrance, I impulsively grasped the flower with both hands and pressed it into my face, unmindful of a certain buzzing sound. Annoyed at my imper-

tinence, a bee let me have his response —
right on my left hand. The pain was almost
worth it, though. (Do you remember the lilac bush outside of auntie's back porch in
Massachusetts?)

"Every day after lunch, we must walk
for an hour up the road, always in a group.
One day, we came upon a field of buttercups. Enthralled, I reached down to touch
them. 'Oh, buttercups...,' I exclaimed. The
other postulants who were next to me did
not think that it was anything unusual. Immediately, I was six years old again, experiencing the delicious sensation of lying in
the moist morning dew of a summer mead-
ow, face toward the warming sun, watching Skippy chase butterflies through the
fields.

"After we complete our morning chores
each day, we are assigned to academic
classes. I was a little surprised at this at first,
because I had thought we would go out
with the older sisters to visit the poor. I
guess that was what they did in the 'old
days' but it seems that the superiors of all
various communities have been criticized
for not adequately preparing the nuns —
education-wise — for their various fields of
endeavor. Consequently, there is a very
great emphasis on education now and the

sisters here have even formed their own college.

"Because I have already had some of the
basic courses, I have been assigned to study
mostly sacred theology or philosophy. Most
of the postulants in my band entered right
after high school and a few, like me, had
some education prior to entrance. There is
one, though, a Miss Kelly, who is barely six-
teen and she had to obtain a special dispen-
sation to finish her high school in
Postulatum. She is very sharp and keen-
witted — also very beautiful, with blonde
hair and blue eyes and a true peaches-and-
cream complexion. Even though she's only
two years younger than I, she seems so re-
markably youthful in appearance. They
placed a new and rather somber plaque of
the Madonna in the hallway recently. I was
gazing at it, trying to discover some redeeming feature, when Miss Kelly passed
by and noted with a wry grin, 'Looks like
she's suffering from a mild case of dyspep-
sia, doesn't it?'

"Several of my friends from high school
and college have written — also Mark. I
have tried to explain, in the nicest terms
possible, that I will not be able to corre-
spond with them at all after February first,
when I enter the Novitiate, God willing. I
do hope they will understand.

"The bell has just rung, calling us to prayers. We are constantly told that the bell is the 'voice of God' and we must obey it immediately.

"I pray for you each day at Mass.

Love,
Patricia"

I put down my pen. My family seldom wrote. "It doesn't matter," I lied to myself. No one in our family ever really communicated. Since that day, my mother and I rarely spoke — since that day —

* * * * * * * * * *

Skippy, my dog and beloved companion for ten years, had been hit by a car in the fog one night and died.

At the end of my sophomore year, all the pressures at school and at home bound me until I began to feel claustrophobic. One clash after another between my mother and me intensified the pressure until I felt as though I would explode. The day she began to caustically berate grandmother, I finally did. "Stop it! Stop it!" I screamed. "It's bad enough you're always yelling at the rest of us — I won't allow you to belittle grandmother. She's your own mother!"

Instantly, she reached out and slapped me hard across the face. My hand shot up into the air to strike her back. It felt as though something forcibly held my arm suspended in mid-air for a moment, and then it dropped limply at my side. I was both shocked at the force of my anger and surprised at my inner control that would not allow me to strike my mother.

The next day, I was putting away the linens at the nursing home which my parents owned. I had worked there since

39

it opened. Observing that I had done it incorrectly, my mother, in front of all the nurses, said to me with dripping sarcasm, "You aren't worth the salt you're made of!"

To me this was the final blow in a long series of verbal assaults. Something inside of me snapped. I recall one of the nurses holding on to me long enough to whisper in my ear, "Don't let it get to you, honey, she's just jealous of you," and she swore at my mother under her breath.

The next thing I remember, I was sitting in an orange grove, panting from running pell-mell as far as my legs would carry me. "I've got to get out — I've got to get out!" The words rang in my pounding head, as I whimpered like a wounded animal.

"God, let me die. I need to die." Slowly I realized what my mind was screaming. Gripped with the icy realization of my thoughts, I forced them from my sorrow-filled mind. Suicide is a mortal sin. I would go to hell, forever! And yet, I needed to sleep. Maybe if I slept for a long, long time, the pain of my life would soften into a dim and distant dream.

I waited until the 11 p.m. shift change at the nursing home. Slipping into the nurses' station I went to the medicine cabinet and quickly unlocked it, grabbed a handful of sleeping pills and swallowed them.

The events that followed are hazy in my memory. I can remember mother alternately hitting me in the face and trying to force black coffee down my throat. Her words scalded me as much as the hot coffee, "I won't let you do this to me! I won't let you disgrace me!" She screamed the words over and over until I lapsed into unconsciousness.

From the darkness of sleep, I heard grandmother saying in a calm but very firm voice, "Alice, if you don't stop hitting that child, I'm going to call the police."

Feeling a sharp prick in my arm, I roused with a start. Mother had just given me a shot of something. Through my blurred vision I saw her hurry from the room. Standing next to me was grandmother. "Nama," I whispered thickly, "as soon as I get through sleeping, we'll get a car and go back to Connecticut, okay?"

Her eyes filled with tears. Taking a handkerchief from her pocket, she covered her mouth to stifle the sobs that erupted from deep within her.

As slumber overcame me again, I thought, "I've never seen grandmother cry before."

* * * * * * * * * *

After supper, on the evening of January 31, the Mother General, head of the Western Province, called us together:

"Tomorrow, immediately after Mass and breakfast, you will be escorted over to the Novitiate wing of the Motherhouse. There you will begin your year of canonical novitiate.

"I cannot stress too greatly how important this year is in the formation of a Sister of Charity. You are to take all of your thoughts off of everything of this world and concentrate only on God. With the exception of your daily walk together after lunch, you will maintain strict silence at all times unless a superior asks you a question.

"During the coming year, you will not study any secular subjects — just theology and sacred music. You will be constantly instructed and exercised in all areas pertaining to poverty, chastity and obedience. These are the three vows which you will be permitted to take, on a temporary basis, at the end of the year — provided the community finds you worthy of doing so.

"There will be days when you will want to give up, but never, never give in to that cry of your lower nature. Remember, feelings don't count; sanctity lies in the will. If you lose your vocation, you just may very well lose your soul.

"You are a rather unusual band, in that there were twenty-six who entered nine months ago and none have left. May you continue to persevere. God bless you."

Forming two rows of thirteen, walking somberly on each side of the corridor, we crossed the hallowed threshold of the Novitiate the next morning. There to greet us, with two assistants, was Sister Rebecca, Mistress of Novices. "Good morning, sisters. You will now be ushered to your alcove in the dormitory. After closing the curtains, take off ALL articles of clothing which you are now wearing and place them on the bed. Put on the clothing you will find on the chair. If you need assistance, wave your hand outside of the curtain and an older novice will come to help you. Remember, all of this is to be done in absolute silence."

We were given first a full-length, white linen chemise, worn next to the body; over that was a simple laced vest; then a floor-length, black wool dress; a linen shawl pinned at the waist; on our heads, first a scull cap to completely hide our hair and then a white linen "coif" that protruded all around, cutting off all peripheral vision.

As I proceeded with the dressing, I began to hear muffled giggles. Then, somewhere from above, I heard a soft, but distinct, "Psst!" Looking up, I observed that Miss Schmidt, from Dallas, had lifted her nose and incredulous eyes over the curtain of my alcove. She whispered, "Mercy, are y'all missing any certain articles of underwayah?"

Before she could continue, the Novice Mistress pulled open her curtains and angrily rebuked her, "Sister, get down off of that bed immediately. We never stand on our beds, and we never, ever speak in the dormitory. You have already broken two important rules. Do you want to leave right now?"

"No, mother, I'm very sorry." Sister Schmidt kissed the floor. She would be assigned her penance later.

Was this, then, the "great secret" of the Novitiate? Were we to forego even the convenience of twentieth-century underclothes in our pursuit of ancient asceticism?

There was, in fact, much more to come. We were allowed only one bath per week and that with carbolic soap. Nothing dainty or scented was ever permitted. We would wash our hair only once per month with the same harsh soap. Deodorant was forbidden. (No wonder the professed sisters used to joke about the "odor of virtue" whenever a novice approached them.) Why were all of these vestiges of medieval monasticism required of us? We were incessantly reminded that we had to punish our body and bring it into subjection. All of these self-imposed rigors fell into the category known as "mortification of the flesh." The major premise was that if the body was brought into complete control, the soul would soon follow.

Unlike the rectangular arrangement of the Postulatum community room, the novices sat at long benches or pews, facing each other (but never looking directly at each other), Quaker-style, with an aisle down the middle. At one end of the open passageway, there was a small altar, with a statue of Mary, and at the other end presided the Novice Mistress. Twice a day, once in the morning and again in the evening, we would be brought into this room for instruction in the Rule. The Novice Mistress would read the Rule to us or explain it while we listened in silence, doing our personal sewing or darning. (I darned the same black stocking for six months.)

Usually the exhortations were dull and repetitious, such as, "The sisters shall never question their superiors. They shall render blind obedience to the one placed over them, as to the Lord himself. When they are directed to do something by a superior, they must do it without question, and in a spirit of true humility."

Every once in a while, one of the other community administrators would take the Novice Mistress' place and give the instruction. My favorite was Sister Assistant, the second-in-command to the Reverend Mother. Sister Assistant had been a teacher and school principal for many year and she seemed to have more of a down-to-earth attitude than either the Novice Mistress or Reverend Mother, both of whom had been hospital administrators. The hospital sisters were known to be more staid and reserved than the teachers or social workers.

One day, after she finished reading part of the Rule pertaining to the vow of poverty: "The sisters shall remember that they have no property of their own, and that everything belongs to the community and is merely given to them for their temporary use," Sister Assistant went on with her remarks. "Well, I want to tell you, I've run across some sisters who have really made me wonder why they come here at all. To look at them, you'd think they were 'queen bees' or something. They act like they own the place. I think they must have said to themselves, 'To work, I am unable; to beg, I am ashamed. I know what I'll do, I'll join the Sisters of Charity!'"

Another time she had read part of the Rule regarding chastity: "The sisters shall be careful never to allow anyone to touch them, and they shall avoid all particular friendships. If they feel that another sister or person is particularly attracted to them, they shall inform their superior immediately." Shaking her head, she sighed, "Now I've got to tell you that I've seen some mighty peculiar things in the past thirty years or so. I can halfway understand when one of our women leaves on the arm of a man. That shouldn't be, but it happens if you don't obey the Rule. But for the life of me, I can never fathom why a woman would leave on the arm of another woman — that just beats all, in my book!"

I tried to keep my eyes on my much-darned sock, but my shoulders shook with repressed laughter. "This is one woman I'd really like to get to know someday," I thought.

For some, the total silence was the greatest burden to bear. Often I would go up to the fourth-story attic where we washed and hung out our stockings and find two sisters frantically whispering. "I can't stand this silence. If I don't talk to somebody soon, I'm gonna' burst," I remember one novice crying to a sympathetic soul. I tried to keep the Rule governing silence, as I did all the others.

The half hour of recreation when we had to either walk with or sit next to two other sisters whom we barely knew and "converse" only on edifying subjects —I found this to be more difficult than the silence. At least in the silence, I would be alone with my own real thoughts.

Night after night, we could hear muffled sobs as sisters cried themselves to sleep, each in her own private misery. How strange, never to reach out a hand of sympathy or compassion. That was forbidden. Each must undergo her own ordeal absolutely alone.

On our walk one day in the spring, I noticed that the daffodils were blooming, and I remembered that it had been just about a year ago that I had told Mark, "If I'm not back within one year don't wait for me. Make a life for yourself...."

* * * * * * * * * *

Shortly after my sixteenth birthday, one Friday evening I attended a Catholic Youth Organization meeting for Orange County. There I met Mark, who was to play a very special role in my life. He was darkly handsome, with sparkling hazel eyes and a gleaming, warm smile. Unlike the other boys I knew, he didn't attend Loyola High School, or St. Anthony's. He was a "public" from Anaheim High School. He had a gentle, wry sense of humor and we became fast friends, instantly.

The following Monday, as we prepared for dismissal, I looked out the classroom window. I could hardly believe my eyes. There was a shiny, black Chevy parked right in front of Marywood. "Now that takes nerve," I thought to myself as I skipped down the steps to join him.

Sensing the multitude of curious eyes peering at him from the ivy-covered edifice, he quipped, "Up, periscope!" We both collapsed in laughter.

Mark brought great joy and sanity into my life at a time when I desperately needed both. He was one of the kindest, most affable persons I'd ever known.

At first I was afraid he would be offended by mother's switch-blade tongue, but he shrugged and said, "Hey - don't worry about it. I'll just overwhelm her with kindness and charm." And he did.

*   *   *   *   *   *   *   *   *   *

A strange melancholy overtook me which I couldn't seem to shake. At evening prayers I said, "O God, take this terrible ache from my heart. I *will* to let Mark and everything in my past go. Forgive my weak feelings."

Would this tremendous, overwhelming oppression, this sense of total alienation, ever diminish? Would the renunciation of all earthly love, all ordinary satisfaction and fulfillment ever bring any true peace? Would my restless heart ever find rest in God?

Having only questions, no answers, I relentlessly kept searching.

4

Prenuptial Penance

*"For I know the plans that I have for
you," declares the Lord, "plans for
welfare and not for calamity to give you
a future and a hope.
"Then you will call upon Me and come and
pray to Me, and I will listen to you.
"And you will seek Me and find Me, when
you search for Me with all your heart."*
(Jer. 29:11-13)

"The Bride of Christ...." This was my aim, my goal
— I must keep that before me at all times. At the end of
this year, I would be permitted that most glorious of all
privileges — to become married to Christ, to exchange
my worthless life for one with Him, in a mystical union
— vowing not to a human spouse but to an unseen Lord,
to be forever without earthly possessions, chaste, obedi-
ent.

I paid no attention to my aching knees, already sore from hundreds of hours of prayer, as I bent over and polished the long hardwood corridor connecting the central wing of the Motherhouse to the Novitiate. I tried to keep my thoughts uplifted. "It's worth it all. All for thee, Jesus."

A terrible commotion broke through the customary stillness. From the front visitors' parlor, a man was shouting, "I've come to take my daughter out of this prison! Where is she? I want her right now! See these clothes! I brought her an entirely new wardrobe and I'm gonna' spread every single article out right here in this stuffy room!"

("Oh, dear! What do I do? Do I keep polishing? Do I leave? I'm under obedience to finish this hallway...." I just kept my rag moving and my head down.)

Suddenly, the Reverend Mother scurried down the main staircase, accompanied by two other nuns. "I'll take care of this, Sister Beata," she motioned to the sister who was assigned to greeting visitors.

"Hah! You must be the warden. You look like one!" the man exclaimed.

("Heavens, doesn't that man know that you never speak to nuns like that! That borders on blasphemy." I half-expected the ground to open and swallow him up.)

"Your daughter is just fine, Mr. Anderson," Reverend Mother replied calmly. "She's in the Novitiate now and not allowed to have any visitors."

"Oh, yeah? Unless you want me to come back with my shotgun, you'd better get her right now," and he swore at her.

After a rustle of skirts and beads, the Novice Mistress appeared with a petite, white-faced novice whom I had only seen once or twice during recreation periods. She had entered before me and was due to make her profession in about a month.

In a barely audible voice she offered, "Daddy, I'm fine. Really I am."

"Listen, Mary Ellen" he bellowed. "I want you to take off that ridiculous outfit and those horse blinders. You look like that character on the Dutch cleanser can! Put on these nice clothes I brought you, and come home with me right now! Your mother may be Catholic, but I'm not and I refuse to put up with this nonsense any more. I even bought you a brand-new car and drove it all the way from Evansville. Take a look at it, honey, it's your favorite color — blue!"

The last voice I heard was that of Reverend Mother, speaking in a conciliatory tone, "I'm sure we can discuss this sensibly —"

At that point the Novice Mistress noticed me. She was visibly shaken, "Sister Nolan, what are you doing there?"

"My assignment, mother."

"Oh — oh — all right. You may go back to the Novitiate now. Do not ever speak of anything you may have overheard."

The next day, at Mass, I watched as the tiny form of Sister Anderson knelt at the communion rail. Her frail shoulders were trembling slightly; she was probably crying. I was surprised that she was still there. Whenever a sister left, it seemed that she was just "spirited away."

No one ever said anything. They just did not appear at Mass and there was an empty place at the refectory table, leaving an ominous impression on the rest of us.

I tried to concentrate on the wafer melting on my tongue, but my mind wandered.

* * * * * * * * * *

A resounding clang of the impenetrable steel door which I erected around my heart was the only thing that I was conscious of as I stared at the ceiling. Never again would I allow my mother to hurt me. Never again would I allow myself to care about anything she said or did. Never again would I allow myself to feel such searing pain.

"I'm going to say a series of words now. Please give me an immediate, one-word response." From deep within the thick mental fog that surrounded me came these words from a female voice. Mother had admitted me to a private psychiatric clinic in Beverly Hills, far enough away from home so that her acquaintances would not know of the flaw in our "perfect" family.

My mind yelled at the female voice, "Lady, I know all about your tests. I've studied the whole lot of them on my own — the word association; the Thematic Apperception; the Rorschach. I can play these games and fool all of you." Instead, without interrupting my upwardly fixed gaze, I quietly sighed, "This won't do any good, you know."

"Why not, do you think?"

"Because, unless you give my mother the same tests, you'll never really understand the root of the problem. If you get her to agree to take them, then I'll answer your questions."

After several moments of silence, the female voice said, "You really hate your mother, don't you?"

"I suppose."

"*And you also hate your father.*"

Aghast, I finally looked at the voice for the first time. A chic, sophisticated woman, in an appropriate suit and chignon. Her eyes remained steady. She registered no reaction to my horrified look. "*Uh, no, I don't hate my father. I —, I —*"

"*Perhaps because you think that he should not let your mother dominate him. Maybe you expected him to help you — to stand up for you, but he didn't,*" she ventured.

"*I'm tired. I just want to sleep now,*" and I turned to the wall and pulled the covers up over my head.

The resolution to lock my mother out of my life had brought with it a certain calm. I let it be known that I would not go home with her, so my father came to drive me back to Orange. As he lifted my suitcase into the car, I turned to him directly, because I knew that once we were on our way, he wouldn't be able to read my lips. Over the years, he had gradually lost his hearing and become ever more withdrawn. For the first and only time in my life, I posed the question, "*Dad, why don't you stop her — especially when you know that she's wrong? Why don't you do something when she hurts others?*"

After a brief pause, he softly said, "*Well, I figure I knew what she was like when I married her, and I can't change my mind now. I made a vow and I've got to keep it.*" So that's the way it was, and that's the way it always would be. We rode home in silence.

Was he also deaf to my soul's scream of agony? "*Won't you touch me just once? Tell me that you understand, that I'm not a terrible person, that you love me.*"

He remained a shadow in my life.

* * * * * * * * * *

53

In the chapel that morning knelt two young novices softly weeping — one for a father she had left; the other for a father she never had.

When it came time for Sister Anderson's band to leave the Novitiate and receive the full habit, she was not among them. Like so many others, no mention was ever made regarding what had happened to her.

I wondered if the other members of my band took the same mental tally that I did each day — twenty-six at Mass — twenty-six in the refectory — twenty-six at evening prayers. "O God, give us strength...keep us going...."

On those evenings after supper when we did not practice Latin chants with the choir director, we were permitted to read certain, approved spiritual books. I had already become fascinated with the life of one great sixteenth-century Carmelite nun, Teresa of Avila. I wondered that she had managed to maintain her marvelous sense of humor in such austere surroundings. At one point, it was noted, she actually jumped up on the community room table, exclaiming, "My sisters, let us dance with joy to the Lord," and then proceeded to do a flamenco dance.

One of her sisters recounted finding Teresa one day, suffused with light, arms outstretched in front of the cross, apparently talking to the Lord "in unintelligible syllables."

I read a book which she herself had written, entitled, *The Interior Castle*, in which she described the soul's pursuit of holiness in seven stages. Although it had a profound spiritual impact on my life, it was surprisingly filled with a great deal of common sense rather than ambiguous mysticism.

The Practice of the Presence of God by Brother Lawrence also came into my life at this time. This simple lay monk had been assigned the most menial tasks in a French Carmelite monastery. He was not even permitted to say Mass or administer the sacraments. He worked in the kitchen and shoe repair shop, yet he had grasped hold of that all-important principle of dwelling continuously in God's presence and doing everything *in* and *with* Jesus, rather than *for* Him. He never concerned himself with results. (I still read this little gem whenever I feel myself getting caught up in the bustle of the world.)

The excitement which had occurred with Mr. Anderson was certainly atypical of our daily life. Only the change of work assignments broke the monotonous pattern of our routine.

In the middle of August, I was given kitchen duty. At that time, the novices washed and dried all utensils for the entire Motherhouse. I had already broken out in a severe heat rash over my entire body. The oppressive steam from the bins enveloped me and the next thing I knew, I was on the floor. I could hear the nuns discussing me.

"What is wrong with her?"

"I don't know. She's from California — she just can't seem to tolerate the heat too well."

"For heaven's sake, it must get hot in California, too!"

("Not like this," I thought in my bleary mind.)

"Take her to the infirmary."

The infirmary sister, a nurse, shook her head. "You have a terrible heat rash, one of the worst I've ever seen and it's beginning to get infected. Have you told the Novice Mistress about it?"

"No, sister."

"Why not?"

"I — thought — we were supposed to offer up these things in silence, for our sins...."

"Trying to be a great saint, huh? Well, little sister, I'll let you in on a secret. Just *living* in community with a bunch of women is enough of a penance; you don't have to go searching for more. Now, I'm going to give you some ointment, and I'm ordering you to use it. I want to see you next week."

Although she never said so, I believe it was this sister who had me changed from the middle of the crowded dormitory, where it was impossible to catch even a single breath of air at night, to an alcove next to a window. Had she guessed how many nights I had endured my own private purgatory?

"Am I trying to be a great saint?" I asked myself. "Hardly. At the rate I'm going, I'll be lucky if I make it out of purgatory and into heaven at all."

There is an enormous burden of guilt and apprehension accompanying a theology that is based almost entirely on your own good works and lacks the assurance of justification by faith.

God becomes a very fearsome, anxiety-producing entity who looks over your shoulder ready to condemn: "Aha, another venial sin, that means fifty more days in purgatory for you." This may have been the basis of our always seeking for some intermediary to go between us and God. If you want a favor from someone and you are really afraid to ask him directly, to whom would you go? Well, his nice, kind mother, of course — or maybe his stepfather or his friend. If the church had determined, through the involved processes of beautification, then canonization that someone such as St. Vincent de Paul had made it to heaven, why not ask him to intercede for you?

As children, we actually thought that the nuns' prayers were better than ours and that the priests' prayers were even more powerful yet. After all, the priests were always there — in the confessional, on the altar, at the sickbed — somehow going between our sinful, unworthy selves and a perfect, holy, but (we thought) unapproachable God — bringing our petitions to Him and His blessing, in turn, to us.

Now, here I was, soon to be a nun myself, yet I didn't feel that I was much closer to God at all. Would all my self-denial, prayers and penances ever make me holy?

The lack of daily hygiene, combined with the ghastly heat and humidity, also caused some severe cases of acne. With a heavy heart, I watched as Sister Kelly's flawless peaches-and-cream complexion turned to an inflamed, pock-marked red. She would bear these scars for the rest of her life.

Once a week, we had a "Chapter of Faults" during which we confessed our exterior infractions of the Rule to the entire Novitiate (interior sins or faults were only confessed to the priest). Kneeling in front of the Novice Mistress, we would ask pardon for our faults and wait for the public reprimand and penance.

In the refectory I sat directly across from a very sweet novice who apparently had a difficult time with oatmeal which we had almost every morning during the winter months. Breathing deeply, she would place a spoonful of oatmeal in her mouth, then quickly gulp some water, trying hard not to grimace. Every week she would ask pardon for not finishing her oatmeal, and every week she would be told the same thing, "Sister, you simply cannot give in to your flesh like that. You will eat all of your oatmeal, and you will eat it joyfully, thanking God for it." I still see that novice's face whenever I eat oatmeal.

As it had since my earliest years, the predictable cycle of the church year and the rhythm of the liturgy offered me a sense of certainty which was lacking in my personal life.

During Lent all of the vestments were purple and the Latin chants took on a mournful tone. One of the functions of the Lenten season was the Stations of the Cross. I found a vague sort of comfort in walking with Christ along the *Via Dolorosa,* The Sorrowful Way. Since Jesus suffered, maybe He could understand my own anguish. I walked these stations often, even when it wasn't the Lenten season.

From Passion Sunday until Easter, all of the statues were covered with purple drapes; the total effect was gloom. This made the Easter vigil service all the more moving and dramatic. In the middle of a completely darkened church, the priest would light the single, large Paschal candle while he chanted, *"Lumen Christi"* (light of Christ), to which we responded, *"Deo Gratias"* (thanks be to God). We then passed the flame around until each of the candles which we held was lighted. All the lights were turned on; banks of lilies were placed around the altar; the organ, which had been silent for six weeks, resounded; the bells pealed — "Christ is risen!"

Advent, the four weeks prior to Christmas, was devoted to preparation for the birth of Christ, which we celebrated with great enthusiasm at midnight Mass.

This year the celebration of Christmas meant more than just the acknowledgment of Christ's birth; it meant that I had only about six weeks left in the Novitiate. Because Christmas is a major holy day, we were allowed to talk at the main meal. Sister Chenizky, a member of my band from a close, Polish family in Chicago, smiled across the table at me, "We all seem to have made it thus far, thank God."

"Yes, we're a surprisingly tough bunch, aren't we?" I replied.

Shortly after Christmas, I was at Mass one morning when I underwent a type of spiritual encounter which almost defies description. As the priest broke the bread and said, in Latin, "This is my body, broken for you...," I looked up at the crucifix above the altar and the words seemed to echo throughout my entire being: "for you...for you...."

At that moment, I felt as though I was lifted out of myself and I knew that I knew that I knew that Jesus had died on Calvary for *me*. Something extraordinary had happened in my spirit, but there were no words to adequately explain it. Catholic theology did not include any such terms as "born again" or "justification," but God is certainly not limited to human theological terms, is He?

(How presumptuous we are to think that we can con-
fine the infinite creativity of the Creator to the repetition
of four spiritual "laws" on a paper card.)

When I left the chapel that morning, I was filled with
a sense of awe. I knew that Jesus Christ was indeed the
Son of God and that He loved me enough to die for me.
There was no audible voice, nor was it the result of any
human exhortation. It was, quite simply and wonderfully, a sovereign move of God. An infinitesimal particle of
God's life and truth had reached down, not because of
the religious structure, but almost in spite of it, and
touched my heart. God has promised, *"And you will seek
me and find me, when you search for me with all your heart"*
(Jer. 29:11-13). He makes no mention of where or how
that shall occur — only that it *shall*.

For over twenty years, I did not ever speak of this to
anyone. As I previously mentioned, there simply were
no words. In reading about the lives of various saints, I
noticed that several of them had referred to something
called "First Love," so I presumed that this must be what
I was experiencing. Everything — whether the most menial task or severe penance — became a great joy. I wanted to give back to Jesus some tiny portion of the love I
had received. I wanted, above all else, to prepare for my
soon-coming marriage to Him.

On January 31, the Reverend Mother again assembled our band: "My dear sisters, the day after next, February second, you will mark forever in your memories
as your wedding day. On that day, you will receive the
full habit of the Sisters of Charity, and you will make
vows of poverty, chastity and obedience to our Lord

Jesus Christ, through the Holy Mother Church. This is a very solemn occasion. For the next two days, you will be relieved of all duties so that you can concentrate on the tremendous commitment you are about to make. You will also be asked to submit to the Novice Mistress the name which you would like to be referred to in religious life. It should be the name of our Blessed Mother or a canonized saint, and no other sister in this province should have it.

"Tomorrow, you will undergo, in absolute silence, the monastical ceremony known as tonsure. Your hair will be cut off as a sign of your humility and your total withdrawal from the world."

She then smiled slightly, "You are somewhat of a miracle band in the community. There are still twenty-six of you. God bless you...."

That evening, as I took off my white skull cap, my hair cascaded down around my shoulders. I thought of the young women who had come in with really long, lovely hair. Theirs must be down to their waists by now. "Oh, well," I thought, "no big loss for me. At least I'll be able to take a daily shower again soon — and wash, literally, from stem to stern." Losing my hair did not bother me that much. I had always thought of myself as homely, anyway.

* * * * * * * * * *

No picture of me graced the piano or mantelpiece. There was one large photograph of my sister, as a baby, on the hall table. My papers were never displayed, nor even acknowledged, neither were my report cards or special awards.

An incident impressed itself forcibly on me when I was seven, setting an image in my mind that would profoundly affect me in the future.

It was Christmas and Uncle Will and auntie were visiting us. I asked mother why there was no baby picture of me on the hall table. Curtly, she responded, "Well, there was a Depression and we just couldn't afford it."

Uncle Will, who had imbibed too much whiskey at that point, added, "Maybe you were too ugly." Everyone in the room, including my sister, parents and even my grandmother, laughed. I burst into tears and ran from the room.

That night, and many nights thereafter, I cried myself to sleep thinking, "Maybe that is why no one loves me. I must be ugly."

* * * * * * * * * *

The next day, we were gathered in one side parlor. We sat in silence in a circular arrangement. No one had said even a word to us. From the adjacent room we could hear, "Bzzzt. Bzzzt. Bzzzt."

Although I was trying to keep my eyes cast modestly down at first, curiosity got the better of me and I stole a glance around the room. Most were rather somber. Sister Kilgallon had two large tears silently cascading down her cheeks. Sister Kelly, like me, struck with the surrealism of the situation, was trying to restrain a grin. Suddenly, Sister McKensie jumped to her feet and screamed, "I can't stand it! I can't stand it!" and she bolted down the hallway, crying hysterically, with two nuns in hot pursuit.

"Oh, no," I thought. "You can't give up now, McKensie — not after all we've been through. It's only hair!"

Just then the Novice Assistant tapped me on the shoulder and beckoned me to follow her. Placing a cape around my neck, she began with the scissors first, then came the clippers, "Bzzzt. Bzzzt."

We were not allowed mirrors, because that was considered vanity. When I was alone, I could not resist polishing the brass doorknob with my sleeve and taking a peek. Absolutely all gone!

The next morning, when I saw Sister McKensie sitting at her usual place at breakfast, I wanted to throw my arms around her and tell her how glad I was to see her. Instead, I broke into a huge grin and nodded, as if to say, "Atta girl! You made it!"

It wasn't until two years later that I found out that poor Sister McKensie had been all through Postulatum and Novitiate *before*, and had gone home at that exact same moment — the tonsure ceremony. She had to repeat the entire, torturous year and nine months all over again.

I had been so excited about seeing Sister McKensie, that I failed to notice the simple white card which had been placed on top of my plate — the succinct proclamation of my future life:

"Sister Augusta Nolan"

5

Send My Roots Rain

Unless the Lord builds the house,
They labor in vain who build it;
Unless the Lord guards the city,
The watchman keeps awake in vain.
It is vain for you to rise up early
To retire late, To eat the bread of
painful labors;
For He gives to His beloved even in
his sleep.

(Ps. 127:1,2)

Because of the emphasis on education, all of the sisters went immediately from the Novitiate to the juniorate for their college degrees and "formation." It was a far cry from Vincent de Paul's original ideal of sisters working with the poor.

Next to the turn-of-the-century sprawling edifice known as the Motherhouse, the community erected a

65

modernistic, anachronistic glass building which became Marillac College. An article was published in *The Catholic Digest* which described our training center as "West Point for Sisters," and indeed it was just that. All the nuns, regardless of their designated fields of teaching, social work or nursing, had to earn not only bachelor degrees, but also acquire the equivalent of minors in Catholic theology and philosophy. It was here that we were introduced to Thomas Aquinas, the undisputed luminary of Catholic theologians. It was said that Aquinas "baptized" Aristotle, as Augustine had "baptized" Plato, utilizing their respective, philosophical methods to teach Catholic doctrine. Although, like most Catholics, I stood in awe of the brilliant intellect of Aquinas, I personally never thought he had the heart of Augustine.

The college was the dream of Sister Bernadette who, I discovered, had earned one of the first Ph.D.'s in the community. Like everything from our past, degrees were never supposed to be alluded to. In order to staff it, they had brought in from all the states the most educated nuns of our own order, as well as other communities, and several priests from St. Louis University. It struck me as rather incongruous that an order specifically designated to serve the poor would be pouring enormous amounts of money into such an endeavor.

There also seemed to be many other contradictions — such as telling us that we had to obey the Rule which stated that all lights must be out and the sisters in bed by 10:00, but making us carry eighteen units per semester. Sisters were often found holding flashlights under their blankets or hiding in bathrooms or closets as they studied well into the night. To me, such subterfuge made a mockery of the vow of obedience.

The pressures to excel were enormous. (Whatever happened to humility?) One day, when Sister Bernadette announced that they would be instituting a new grading scale, with "A" beginning at ninety-seven percent, I turned to Sister Maria and said, "You've got to be kidding! Whom are we trying to impress?"

Without batting an eyelash, she immediately answered, "The accreditation committee."

"Ah, I see," I responded. "We are the guinea pigs for accreditation."

"Yes, and instead of red badges of courage, we have those blue badges lined up in the refrigerator. You know, the bottles of antacid that people drink like water around here."

Although I couldn't seem to resolve the various conflicts in my own mind, I kept trying to apply myself to the studies and go along with the program. Some of the teachers were excellent. I vividly recall Sister Frances, our child psychology professor. Stopping in the middle of class one day and looking wistfully out the window, she sighed, "My children — how I miss my children." Then she immediately regained her composure and the customary facade of the non-emotional nun. She had founded a home for Down's syndrome children and had been the administrator of the home for many years before being abruptly sent to the college to teach.

There was one nun whom I greatly admired. Her name was Sister Marvella. She was from another order and had been brought to the college specifically to teach

English literature. She did more than instruct us; she birthed in us an appreciation for the well-written word. She gave the impression of great pressure, stretched to the breaking point, but always under strict control.

It was Sister Marvella who first introduced me to the great Jesuit poet, Gerard Manley Hopkins. I can still hear her as she slowly, reverently recited:

God's Grandeur

The world is charged with the grandeur of God.
    It will flame out, like shining from shook foil;
    It gathers to a greatness, like the ooze of oil
Crushed. Why do men then now not reck his rod?
Generations have trod, have trod, have trod;
    And all is seared with trade; bleared, smeared with toil;
    And wears man's smudge and shares man's smell—the soil
Is bare now, nor can foot feel, being shod.

And for all this, nature is never spent;
    There lives the dearest freshness deep down things;
And though the last lights off the black West went
    Oh, morning, at the brown brink eastward, springs —
Because the Holy Ghost over the bent
    World broods with warm breast and with ah! bright wings.

Who was this man, this priest, with such a marvelous gift for expressing the individual nature of God's creation, as well as the intensity of his own inner life? By the time Sister Michelle finished reading a second poem, *Pied Beauty*, I was smitten.

Glory be to God for dappled things —
    For skies of couple-color as a brindle cow;
        For rose-moles all in stipple upon trout that swim;

Fresh-firecoal chestnut-falls; flinches' wings;
   Landscape plotted and pieced — fold, fallow, and plow;
   And all trades, their gear and tackle and trim.

All things counter, original, spare, strange;
   Whatever is fickle, freckled (who knows how?)
   With swift, slow; sweet, sour; adazzle, dim;
He fathers-forth whose beauty is past change —
   Praise Him.

Immediately after class, I rushed to the library to find out more about this Victorian poet with whom I felt an instantaneous kinship. Two years after converting to Catholicism, Hopkins had joined the Jesuit order and burned all of his poetry. He did not start to write again until seven years after becoming a priest. The melancholy eyes and finely chiseled features peering back at me from the page bespoke an extremely sensitive soul. Was he, as I, caught between the searing beauty of the Creator's imprint on this world and the excruciatingly painful alienation of having to live in it? When I read that he had died at the age of forty-five, I was actually relieved. He had been released.

There alone in the corner of the library, I read:

Thou Art Indeed Just, Lord

Thou art indeed just, Lord, if I contend
With thee; but, sir, so what I plead is just.
Why do sinners' ways prosper? and why must
Disappointment all I endeavor end?
Wert thou my enemy, O thou my friend,
How wouldst thou worse, I wonder, than thou dost

> Defeat, thwart me? Oh, the sots and thralls of lust
> Do in spare hours more thrive than I that spend,
> Sir, life upon thy cause. See, banks and brakes
> Now, leaved how thick! laced they are again
> With fretty chervil, look, and fresh wind shakes
> Them; birds build — but not I build; no, but strain,
> Time's eunuch, and not breed one work that wakes.
> Mine, O thou lord of life, send my roots rain.

I was not even aware that I was crying until I saw the marks on the page before me. For the next few months, day and night, at meditation, at Mass, at prayers, in class, my mind echoed with Hopkins's plea: "Mine, O thou lord of life, send my roots rain."

You have to have lived with hundreds of women at one time in order to appreciate such a tension producing environment. Unless you've experienced this compression, it literally defies description. The old metaphor, "pressure cooker," seems appropriate.

Sister Marvella and I were alone in the classroom one afternoon. She had asked me to go over some lesson plans with her. As we were leaving, she took my hand and, pressing it to her cheek, she whispered, "You have a beautiful soul."

I was startled at the display of affection, but also flattered that this woman of great learning and depth would care for me in a special way. Her troubled, black eyes bespoke an intense, inner agony. She reminded me of a fragile, caged bird and I longed to set her free.

That was as close as I ever came to a serious involvement with a woman. The intensity of my attraction to her surprised me. It did help me to understand how a soulish bond can form innocently enough and then descend to the physical level.

At the end of the summer session, we parted and I later learned that she had been hospitalized for "a nervous condition." We lost contact after that.

Two years ago, I was speaking with another former sister who referred to homosexuality as the "disease" of nuns and priests. The implication was that most of these men and women in regular, heterosexual living conditions would have behaved "normally." Strange manifestations of sublimation appeared as acceptable in our midst. Sisters would write little verses of affection to each other, leave bouquets of flowers on their nightstands, inscribe books of poetry and place them under their pillows, etc. Most of this was relatively innocent, I suppose, considering the peculiarity of our situation. Sometimes it became more serious.

One day, I came upon two sisters huddled in a corner, holding hands and gazing into each other's eyes. Embarrassed at encountering such an intimate tête-à-tête, I immediately turned and started to leave. What I hadn't noticed was Sister Bernadette at my heels. Her face flushed red and she angrily yelled at the older one, "Listen, Sister R., I didn't bring in all these young sisters to the juniorate so that you could play `footsie' with them behind closed doors. Cut it out right now or I'll ship you out *fast*!" (Within the community, Sister Bernadette was infamous for her blunt and often caustic speech.)

People frequently ask me if such occurrences were common. Because I avoided these entanglements like the plague, I really don't know the full impact on the community at large. From my limited perspective, they were common enough to cause me some disturbance. When

I left the community, there were several sisters with such propensities who remained in the order, and I often wondered why they were allowed to stay.

As far as my own aversion for such liaisons, in addition to my trying to observe the Rule and the reliving of the abhorrent incident I had experienced in the San Francisco bar, I think there was also a very practical restraint. If I couldn't become "entangled" with a man, I certainly wasn't going to do so with a woman.

One morning we had a Requiem Mass for a sister who had recently died. She had spent her entire adult life in the community and had celebrated her Golden Jubilee (fiftieth year) ten years before I had entered. It was said that she had served the poor faithfully until her peaceful departure from this world. As the nuns chanted the mournful *"Dies Irae"* (day of wrath, day of woe....), I resolved for the first time in three years to speak about what had been weighing heavily on my mind.

Immediately after breakfast, I went to the Sister Superior of the juniorate, Sister Genevieve.

"Do you need to see me right now, Sister Augusta?" She looked a little perturbed.

"Yes." The firmness in my voice caught her off-guard.

"Oh — what is it?"

"Sister, I've been thinking for a long time that I'm doing the same thing now that I was doing back home."

"Which is?"

"Going to school full-time."

"Yes, well?"

"Well, that's not what I came to do, you know. I really thought I'd be working with the poor and my heart just isn't in this."

"I'm really surprised, Sister Augusta. You're one of our best students. Besides, it's your *will* that has to be in it."

"That may be, but I'm not really accomplishing what I set out to do, and I don't see any point in it."

"Well, this is really a disappointment, but I'll talk to Reverend Mother about it." She dismissed me curtly.

I then went to class, not really sure what would come of that brief conversation, but feeling relieved that I had spoken. The next morning after Mass, Sister Genevieve tapped me on the shoulder and beckoned me to follow her into her office.

Primly, she began, "Sister Augusta, you will pack your things today and be ready tomorrow morning to leave for your new assignment. You are being missioned to Guardian Angel Settlement House, downtown St. Louis." Then giving me a rather disparaging look, she added, "You'll be working with the very *poorest* of the poor."

My joy was not unalloyed as the word spread to the other sisters that I was leaving. "Gus, what did you do? How did you tell them? *What* did you tell them?"

"I don't know — just how I felt."

Not a few remarked, "Good for you, Gus. God bless you."

Sister Annette Kelly said it best: "Just think, Gus, you're going to be with real, live *people!*"

Lying in bed that night, I couldn't sleep as I told myself, incredulously, "Tomorrow!" Why so soon? I had not been summoned to speak with any of the chiefs — just quickly missioned out. Then it dawned on me that keeping me around, after I had made known my thoughts, would probably have been dangerous. After all, I just might undermine the entire juniorate program and cause a mass exodus. For the first time in months, I actually chuckled to myself.

Sister Bernadette never spoke to me after that. I later found out that she had considered me one of her protégés and when I criticized the juniorate program, her "baby," she had taken it personally. Sometimes we would see each other at annual retreats, but she always turned away. Today we would refer to her as a "type A" personality — relentlessly driving herself and everyone around her. Eventually she became so completely involved in the program that she literally burned herself out — mentally and physically. After years of battling manic-depressive psychosis, she died of a heart attack.

Marillac College no longer exists today. The buildings were purchased by the state university years ago. Whenever I think of Sister Bernadette, I am always reminded of a singular, significant ceremony which is carried out in the presence of every new pope immediately before he ascends to the throne. An acolyte lights a candle, then blowing it out, he says directly to the pontiff, *"Sic transit gloria mundi."* ("Thus passes the glory of the world.")

6

Good Works in the Ghetto

Then the righteous will answer Him, saying,
"Lord, when did we see You hungry, and feed
You, or thirsty, and give You drink?
"And when did we see You a stranger, and
invite You in, or naked, and clothe You?
"And when did we see You sick, or in prison,
and come to You?
And the King will answer and say to them,
"Truly I say to you, to the extent that you
did it to one of these brothers of Mine, even
the least of them, you did it to Me."
(Matt. 25:37-40)

Nothing in anything I'd ever read or heard prepared me for the reality of the ghetto. Driving just a few miles across the city from the Motherhouse, I entered a world of stark misery and bleakness like that which Charles

Dickens described a hundred years before. In the midst of these squalid conditions at 1029 Marion Street was the settlement house. With the exception of the preschool playrooms, which were gaily decorated, the structure itself was ancient, gloomy and drafty in winter, sweltering in summer.

To me, what mattered was that these ten women were unselfishly carrying out their ministry to the downtrodden and destitute. Unlike other priests and nuns who went back to their safe suburbs every evening, these sisters lived among those whom they served, sharing the burden of their stigma.

I thought it strange that the Sister Superior, Sister Mary John, did not greet me. The sister who did, Sister Veronica, explained that an epidemic of hepatitis had broken out six months before, killing several people in the area, including two children in the day-care program. Sister Mary John and another sister, Sister Philomena, had contracted it and were still required to rest most of the day. We rarely saw them and I often wondered why they weren't recalled to the Motherhouse to rest and be replaced by healthy sisters. Apparently they didn't want to leave the "real" world. This placed a great burden of extra work on the remaining nuns. I later was informed that I had taken the place of another young sister who had lasted only six months before she asked to be reassigned; the stress had become too much for her.

In those days, there was no such thing as relaxation and the only time we ever had any thing which even approximated a vacation was the annual retreat — a week devoted to prayer, meditation and listening to special speakers, usually Vincentian (our "brother" order) priests. Otherwise, we worked until we dropped — every day of the year, except Sundays which were spent going to two Masses and catching up on all personal necessities.

Sisters were looked upon then as some kind of perpetual machines. We were to keep working, unceasingly, without respite, without complaint. It was expected of "good" nuns. It may be different for other former religious, but the three most difficult things I personally had to contend with were: the loneliness of alienation, the pettiness and friction resulting from living with so many women under claustrophobic conditions and the constant physical and mental exhaustion.

I was the youngest member of the household, and I was assigned to the preschool/day-care department. This proved to be very advantageous for me. Although I had studied child development and psychology and had acquired a bit of theoretical knowledge, working with the children themselves was most beneficial. I began to understand the wisdom of the older nuns who gained their education during summers and Saturdays while continuing to get practical experience in their fields.

Being with children made me acutely aware of what I had given up in relinquishing physical motherhood. I tried to put the thought out of my mind, because it seemed to evoke a terrible emptiness within me. One day Miss Minnie, my aide, asked me directly, "Do you ever regret not having children of your own, sister?" In spite of the constant warnings not to get too close to "seculars," I felt that she had asked an honest question which deserved an honest answer.

"Yes, Miss Minnie, I do. But they tell us that we will have thousands of spiritual children in this life, and in heaven God will give us all the children that no one else wanted." A good, standard response, but it didn't quite satisfy the yearning of my empty womb.

Miss Minnie was big, black, beautiful and *Baptist!* What a novel experience for me. She was always smiling and often humming. One day I asked her, "Miss Minnie, what are you humming?"

"Oh, I jus' *love* to sing to the Lord, you know. I'm in my church choir and never, ever miss a Wednesday or Sunday service or a Thursday practice. Do you all sing too, sister?"

"Well, it's not quite as lively as yours, that's for sure, but I like to hear you. Keep singing."

Sometimes I would look at her and think how church doctrine said that she was among the "unsaved," yet she sure *looked* like she loved Jesus. "Maybe," I thought, "she's never really understood that the Catholic Church is the only true church and she has attained 'Baptism of Desire.' She sure has something!"

Summer brought with it the usual high humidity and interminable heat. At night in my very small room, which was about ten feet square, I would leave the window open while I lay in the dark listening to the sounds of the city. Many times I would not be able to sleep. In addition to the traffic, fighting, swearing, ambulances and police cars, there was a constant annoying, banging sound always coming from the alley below. When I mentioned this to Miss Minnie one day, she gave me a big, toothy grin and said, "You sure ain't no city girl, are you, sister? Those are *rats* jumpin' from can to can, makin' that racket," and she laughed. "You'll get used to it."

She then went on to explain how the children often played a game called "Bat the Rat." While one of them held the lid on a trash can with a trapped rat inside, others would get sticks. On the count of three, the lid would be raised and whoever could bat the rat first was the winner. Things which I found appalling, these young people had accepted as part of everyday life. My heart went out to them.

Once you have come face to face with True Poverty, her ghastly features are impressed forever on your memory. I learned from the children how to "stomp your feet" before entering a darkened room in the housing projects in order to scatter rats and other creatures; never to use elevators because they were too dangerous; never to leave a baby unattended in a crib because the rats would go for his throat. What I learned could fill pages. I received my greatest education there.

Two years after I left Guardian Angel, I met the sister whom I had replaced, the one who had lasted only six months. She approached me with, "How did you ever stand it there? Some of those women were so weird and the work was unbelievably hard."

I don't recall what I said in response. I'm not sure I could even formulate an answer now. I don't know if it was the theology in which I was reared or my Celtic psyche or a combination of both. I only know that I resigned myself to the fact that life on this earth was to be one long purgatory, an endless reparation for my sins. Only in the next life would any true joy or peace be found, for the few who made it.

The trouble was I never really felt that I was "making it." I was always falling short of the Rule, of the standard of holiness set by the saints. It was a spiritual "Catch-22" of sorts resulting in increased anxiety. My only salvation at that time was to lose myself in service to others in this world and somehow hope that it would count in the next.

Within the boundaries of what was permitted, I formed a friendship with only one other nun there. She was from China and her name was Sister Mary. She was an eighty-pound dynamo who had the enviable assignment of being directly in charge of visiting and taking care of the poor. She loved her folks in the projects and they reciprocated. The other sisters told me that she was the only survivor of her Chinese family. I never really asked her for the details, although I wish I had now. She always called me "The Abbess" which I thought strange because I was, in fact, low man on the totem pole. When I asked her why she gave me that nickname, she said, "You look like an 'Abbess' to me. This is what I shall call you."

She had a habit of using metaphors in a way that was truly humorous, such as, "Abbess, I'm in the middle of town, strangled in traffic," or "Just because they're rich people, we're not going to put out the dogs for them...."

One day she approached me very seriously and confided, "Abbess, something has been on my conscience for many years. I want to know what you think." (I wasn't sure that I was up to hearing some sort of deep secret.)

"Well, when I was a little girl, most of the people in my village were Buddhists. There were just a few of us kids who weren't and we hung around together. The people always put the very best food out in front of the statue of Buddha, so we would wait until none of the monks were around and then take it and eat it because — well — we didn't believe in Buddha anyway and the stuff was awfully good to eat. Do you think God has forgiven me for that? Was it a mortal sin?"

Trying to appreciate the seriousness of her dilemma, but only seeing the humor of the innocent prank of these young children, I responded, "Sister Mary, if you think it's so terrible, tell the priest in confession; but all of us have done things in our childhood that we regret, things that were a lot worse than that, too."

At that time I had never actually read the Bible, nor even had one in my hand. I now try to devote part of each day to studying it and, in the course of a year, usually cover it all — from Genesis through Revelation. Each year, when I come across the admonition in Acts 15:29, *"that you abstain from things sacrificed to idols, "* I always smile and ask God to bless Sister Mary.

After she had successfully battled cancer, one of the last things Sister Mary said to me as I was leaving the settlement house for my new mission was, "Abbess, please pray that I go back to my people. I want to die there with them." She is, in fact, in Taiwan now with her "people" and the last I heard she was still very much alive.

During the annual retreat, I was summoned to Sister Assistant's office. She smiled at me, "Well, Sister Nolan." (She always called me by my last name. Perhaps it was because she herself was of Irish descent). "You've

served a three-year exile and done well, I understand."
(Exile — really?) "They haven't let you go to school at
all during that time, have they?"

I wasn't sure who "they" were, but I responded,
"No."

"Have you missed it?"

"The studies, sometimes, but not — "

"Not the juniorate and that whole 'formation' business," she finished for me. Still smiling, she continued,
"Well, you'll get it done soon enough. You just have a
few credits to go and we're going to send you to school
all summer. Then you'll finish part-time, as best you can.
That's how all of us used to do it, you know. It worked
for *us*."

For the first time, I realized that she represented the
"old guard," and she and Sister Bernadette were at opposite poles when it came to how sisters should be
trained and educated.

"So you were hospitalized six months ago. What was
that for, anyway?" (I had the distinct feeling that she already knew.)

"Well, everything the children got, I got — including measles. I guess I didn't have many immunities built
up and —"

"And they also worked you to death there, too, I suppose."

I just nodded. I didn't mention that the doctor had
said the same thing.

"Sister Nolan, we've decided to make a teacher out
of you. At the end of this summer, you will report to St.
Matthias, a new school in the suburbs. You will be teach-

ing sixth grade. I think you'll like it at that small mission. There will only be five of you sisters living at the convent and a couple of lay teachers to help staff the school. You'll be meeting your new superior at the end of retreat. She's a fine woman." Continuing to gaze at me with her piercing, brown eyes, she admonished, "Sister Nolan, I'm counting on you to be one of the very best teachers in the community. You have it in you. I know."

Coming from the pro-of-all-pros, that was the closest I ever got to a compliment from a major superior.

"You don't have to be mean to have good discipline, just *kill* them with a look. Let them know who's boss. Of course, if that doesn't work, you can always try the 'dry knuckle rub' to the head. It doesn't leave any marks either." The same wit that had enlivened the exhortations in the Novitiate shone through.

Averting her eyes for the first time, she gazed into the past as she softly reminisced, "I had some of the best discipline in the community, you know." (Yes, I knew.) "They gave me all the unruly boys — 'juvenile delinquents' — they'd call them today. I shaped them up, and most became fine men —lawyers, doctors, businessmen, even several priests. I still hear from many of them." Coming back to the present, she dismissed me with, "You may go now, sister. I'll be visiting your school one of these days."

Besides Sister Cecilia, my superior at St. Matthias, Sister Assistant, was the only superior I ever had who seemed to take a personal interest in me. Some of the other young nuns were afraid of her, but I liked her.

As the hundreds of sisters who had returned to the Motherhouse for retreat filed into the main chapel that night for prayers, I could not help but wonder which four would be my new companions. Also, the full realization of what had transpired that day hit me.

I had left my beautiful California and dear Sisters of St. Joseph specifically to become a social worker and now I was going to be a teacher anyway. What sort of divine irony was this? Then I remembered that the Rule told us when a superior gave a command, it was the clear manifestation of God's will and must be accepted without doubt or question.

As the sisters began to recite in unison the *"De Profundis"* ("Out of the depths I have cried to thee, O Lord"), all I could think of was, "Send my roots rain." I added my own final entreaty, "Or else I shall surely shrivel up and die."

7

Serving Time in Purgatory

> *My God, my God, why hast Thou forsaken me?*
> *Far from my deliverance are the words of my*
> *groaning.*
> *O my God, I cry by day, but Thou dost not*
> *answer; And by night, but I have no rest.*
>   *(Ps. 22:1,2)*

There is a Scripture verse which says, *"Behold, how good and how pleasant it is for brothers to dwell together in unity"* (Ps. 133:1). This may have been the goal of monastic life for centuries but the fact is, it was seldom realized in actuality.

Throughout my years in community, it was only during my brief tenure at St. Matthias that I experienced anything which even approximated this ideal. A lot was due to the leadership of Sister Cecilia, the superior. Much was made in theory of the superior always leading by example, of being the "servant of all." The reality was often quite the opposite.

Sister Cecilia was the exception. She was a model of integrity and the most humble, self-effacing servant I'd ever encountered. It was largely due to her genuine leadership that our little group of women worked and lived together with relative smoothness and freedom from major problems. For a brief period, my roots received a modicum of rain.

Sister Assistant was right; teaching was my forté. I loved my sixth grade class, but I tried not to show it too much, at least until May. Most of all, it was a treat for me to be with nuns who were not afraid to show that they were genuine people. There was the inevitable friction that always arises whenever women live together in close quarters but with Sister Cecilia's example and guidance, we all worked things out. I had a sincere affection for those four sisters, and I still do.

When I was in the middle of my second year there, Sister Cecilia called me aside and informed me that the community had encountered a difficult situation in a school in Iowa. I had been ordered to replace a nun who had returned "to the world" the previous October. Two lay teachers had tried to take her place, but the class proved unmanageable and they both quit.

I was devastated. Sister Cecilia and I both tried to maintain our self-control in good, soldierly fashion. Only her red eyes betrayed her true feelings. When I returned to the privacy of my room and closed the door, I broke. "Why me? Why, God?" I cried. "Haven't I been good? Haven't I tried to do what was right? Am I being punished because I really like it here? Am I too attached to these students? To this mission?"

The convent at St. Matthias was situated on a hillside adjacent to the school, with a long flight of stairs connecting the house to the asphalt playground below. I had done a rather good job of containing my emotions until, just as I was leaving to get into the car waiting below, I opened the door. There on either side of the walkway, reclining like flowerbeds, were almost all of my former and present students. Many were crying; some were holding each other; several pressed cards and handmade mementos into my hands as I passed. My instinct was to gather them into my arms like a mother hen and assure them, "I love you. I don't want to leave you." Instead, I drew in my breath, re-adjusted my dislodged mask and made it to the car just in time.

I wish I had the gifted pen of Dante to write the remaining part of this chapter, my own personal *"Inferno."* For a long time, the memories were so wrenchingly painful that I completely blocked them out of my consciousness. It has only been very recently that I've been able to acknowledge this portion of my life without risking a rapid descent into depression, and that only by the grace of God. I'm counting on that same grace to assist me in the articulation of this dark episode.

The class that I faced that first day in Iowa was one thing. They were unruly, defiant and boastful about the fact that they had "got rid of" three teachers already. The first impish-faced student who brazenly posed that challenge soon regretted it. Meeting her eyes with a truly murderous stare, I icily challenged, "You may think you're 'hot stuff,' Miss Elliot, but I can assure you that *I am here to stay*. On the other hand, it is *you* who may not make it through the remainder of the year."

One by one, I called each adolescent's bluff. Without giving a centimeter, I systematically held my discipline so firm that they had no choice but to see things my way. I began calling parents, saying that I had initiated a permanent after-school and, if necessary, even Saturday detention program until order was restored.

Most parents responded with, "Great. Keep her as long as you want," or "Terrific, we'll back you up all the way, sister."

One boy who was a notorious troublemaker ended up staying very late one afternoon to do a written assignment because he had disrupted the class. As it got to be about 5:00, he looked up at me and said, "It's getting kind of late, sister."

"Yes," I replied, never lifting my eyes from the papers I was correcting.

About half an hour later, he offered, "Kind of dark outside, isn't it?"

"Yes." I still had not looked at him.

"Should I finish this at home, sister?"

"No, Tim, you are not moving from here until you're done. I can wait all night if necessary."

He finally finished about thirty minutes later, then surprised me by offering to carry my books to the convent about a block away. As he turned to leave for his house, he said, "You're pretty tough, for a nun." He became one of my best students.

Only teachers know how totally draining such an experience can be. The worst part, though, was returning every afternoon to an environment which was much worse than the classroom. Among the thirteen sisters who staffed the elementary and high schools, there was not one that first year who showed me the least bit of kindness or sympathy. I found myself trapped in what turned out to be a notorious cauldron of factions, petty jealousies, competitiveness and downright meanness. Not a few were actually mentally unbalanced.

To stave off depression and utter hopelessness at having to live in this "snake pit," I tried to concentrate all my energies on the classroom. This only made matters worse. The more success I achieved at school and the more popular I became with the parents, the more the older nuns considered me a threat and did everything possible to make life miserable for me.

When parents requested that I take the same class the following year when my present students became seventh graders and then follow them to eighth because I was "the only one who could control them," the elementary principal became infuriated. Because of her incompetence, I was virtually running the school.

Her barely concealed anger took strange forms. Once she told me I had to take yard duty in a veritable blizzard. Clutching my shawl around me and trying to hold my headgear at the same time, I was shivering and my teeth were chattering. An eighth grade girl, seeing my plight, threw her coat over my shoulders and said, "Here, sister, you take this. I'm going in." I later found out that the principal had reported me to a major superior for "worldliness." She told her that I wore a red coat outside.

Often, when I would receive phone calls from parents at the convent, I would hear a "click" during the middle of a conversation, followed by audible sighs and even "tsk-tsks." One nun, whom I shall refer to only as "D," had a very particular friend, "B" (one of several close cliques). One evening, I was in the front parlor speaking with the father of a boy who was having difficulty with his studies. Sister B, opening the door unannounced, peeked her head in and with a ridiculous giggle said, "Aha, Sister Augusta, with one of her gentleman callers. How cute!"

Seeing my consternation, the father quickly assured me, "It's okay, sister. We all know that there are several 'wackos' here and Sister B is one of them."

The lay people all *knew!* What a sham this was! I finally went to the superior of the convent at the end of my second year there and explained how very scandalous this was, for nuns to have such a reprehensible reputation in a small town. She simply nodded and didn't say much. I really thought that she might instigate changes or at least see that some of these nuns with obvious psychological problems received some help. She did nothing.

If you take these few incidents I've briefly described and multiply them times seven, you will get only a fair assessment of one week in the life of a nun in Hades.

When I returned to the Motherhouse in June, I was in a state of spiritual and physical *ennui*. A gray, nameless haze was beginning to overtake me.

Instead of coming in the main gate, the driver took us through the hospital entrance. As I looked over the landscape I saw a female patient with no nurse in attendance. She had a robe and a stocking cap on. "A nun," I thought. "Strange, they usually hide the patients from our view." I noticed that she was smiling broadly and talking — to whom? I bent forward to see — only a tree. As the features became recognizable, my whole being froze. "Oh, dear Lord, it's Sister Marquetta. She's the same age as I am — entered only one year earlier." I said nothing to the other nuns in the car.

Then, as if some odd, tragic drama were being enacted on the stage of my mind, I encountered another strange occurrence almost immediately. After evening prayers, I went back to the chapel just to sit in the dark — alone — or so I thought. There, kneeling in the upper left section usually reserved for the novices, was a professed sister. The first thing I noticed about her was how very thin she was. Her habit was virtually hanging in folds on her. "Who can that be?," I wondered. Then as she genuflected, she turned and slowly moved toward the Novitiate. I thought, "A professed sister going over to the cloistered side? Why?" As I saw her extremely gaunt, silhouetted features, the faintest recollection came to me. It was Sister Jovana, about twenty-eight years old, who had entered the community as a beautiful, robust, rosy-cheeked Indiana farm girl.

When I got to the dormitory, the others were showering or brushing their teeth, preparing for bed — all in absolute silence, of course. I just sat on the edge of my bed and stared at the wall. The sister in charge of the dormitory came over and whispered, "Sister Augusta, what is wrong with you? Are you ill? Why aren't you getting ready for bed?"

All feeling and sensation had drained from me. Dispassionately, almost as if my voice were somehow disconnected from my body, I spoke: "I just saw Sister Jovana. She looks like a skeleton, and they have her hidden on the Novitiate side. What is wrong with her? Why is she over there?"

"First of all, you're not supposed to ask about such matters." She quickly closed the white curtains to shut out the inquisitive glances. "Well, if you *must* know, Sister Jovana is just being very stubborn and prideful. She refuses to eat, and they have her over there so that they can work on getting her to overcome this — this — *pride* of hers. Lights out are in ten minutes. Get ready for bed immediately, Sister Augusta."

I didn't sleep the entire night through. "Refuses to eat? That doesn't sound like the Sister Jovana I used to know." (Later, I found out that when she reached eighty-six pounds, Sister Jovana had been sent home lying on a gurney, with intravenous feeding tubes in her arms.)

At the end of the retreat, I learned that I had been reassigned to Iowa. After the assignments were announced, one of my former companions from St. Matthias said, with tears glistening in her big eyes, "I'm so sorry for you, Gus. You're going back to that 'loony bin.' Just hang on — maybe something will happen. I'll be making novenas for you."

I was beyond hoping that "something" would happen. The bleak fog kept closing in — a general malaise overcame me, depleting me of all caring.

As I began teaching eighth grade that September, I looked at those faces and thought, "These children are my only contact with reality, my reason for going on."

Kneeling at the altar railing one morning in October, I had my hands folded and head bowed, ready to receive communion. Suddenly, just as the priest and the altar boy approached the nun to my right, she started to scream hysterically, crying out with such pitiful wailings that the priest and altar boy looked horrified. As the Superior and another nun lifted her up and removed her from the chapel, Sister Appoliana, who was noted for her indomitable cheerfulness and perpetual smile, was still screaming. They hastily removed her to St. Vincent's Hospital, and we never heard from her again.

A lump formed in my throat that morning that would not go away. All I could think of was how many sisters had gone "over the edge," and my mind kept hammering, *"You are going to be next."*

The nun they sent to replace Sister Appoliana had a very strong, resilient personality. "Listen, Gus, you've got to be *tough*. Don't let those old biddies defeat you. Just think, it's them against us and *we are going to win*. Keep telling yourself that."

Unconsciously, I was smiling at her as she spoke. "Why are you grinning like that, Gus? You're not going to crack up, too, are you? What is it?"

"Oh, it's just — you remind me of someone I knew once. It seems a century ago. She was a lot like you. She told me I had to have *chutzpah*."

Three nights later, this same nun came into my room just as I was getting ready for bed. Placing her finger over her lips to indicate silence, she beckoned me to follow her.

"How peculiar," I mused.

In my nightgown, robe, stocking cap and bare feet, I padded down the darkened hallway behind her.

Stealthily closing the door of her room, she whispered, "Now, Gus, this is a secret — just between you and me — but I'm going to show you something that helps me cope."

To my astonishment, she reached into the back of her closet and withdrew a bottle. My mouth dropped open and I gasped, "How did you ever — "

"Never mind how I got it, just take a swig."

As the sweet, cherry-flavored liqueur warmed my throat, I thought how I never would have broken the Rule like that before. But now I was too numb to care.

I shook my head, "You are really something else."

It was widely known that all the priests had ready access to liquor and, although it was usually kept quiet, many of them were alcoholics.

In our community it was virtually unheard of for a nun to have alcohol in her possession. We could not leave the convent without a companion, and we never carried money unless we were doing an errand for a superior.

"I still can't figure out how you ever — "

"Shhh! Never mind. I've got my ways."

"Amazing." I took another swallow.

"When one of those fruitcakes starts to get to me, I come in here, take a snort and say to myself, 'Listen, lady, long after you're dead and buried, I'm going to be running this community.'"

By this time, I was feeling no pain. As I let out a big hiccup, we both giggled, and I stuffed a pillow over my face to suppress the sound. I was back at Roble Hall again with my friend, Becky. How much alike these two were.

"Gus, you're welcome to come in here anytime and have a drink or two. Just don't tell anyone, O.K.?"

"I really appreciate the offer, but if I start on this stuff, they'll (hiccup) have to carry me out of here. Or worse yet (hiccup), they'll send me to the Funny Farm as a drunk (hiccup), but thanks anyway."

Weaving down the hallway to my room, I thought, "In all this time in Iowa, this is the first nun who ever showed me any compassion at all, and now it's too late."

For months I had cried myself to sleep, but now I could not sleep at all and I could not cry. Most nights I would sit in the darkened chapel with the red, flickering sanctuary lamp as my only companion. Addressing the tabernacle, I would say, "God, they tell me if I leave, I'm going to lose my soul. But if I stay, I'm going to lose my mind."

For the first and only time of my entire life, I could not eat. I would sit at the table and try very hard to get the food down. I could not force it beyond my tightening throat. Whispering and often giggling, the "Bobbsie Twins" would make remarks like, "Ah, Miss America, she must be on a diet," or "Yes, she's watching her figure, has to stay glamorous, you know," and my throat and stomach would constrict tighter.

I knew that I was losing weight at an alarming rate, but I couldn't do anything about it. My background in psychology told me that I was in an anxiety state. The suffocating blackness had become quicksand and I was sinking.

The day after Christmas, I went in to the Superior and told her matter-of-factly, "Sister, I won't be renewing my vows this year on March 25. I thought you should know."

The first thing she said to me was, "Have you told any of the other sisters?"

"No."

Then she said, "Why, sister? Whatever is the problem?"

I thought, "If you don't know by now, I'm certainly not going to try to discuss it," but I answered, "I do not believe in this community life any more. I'm living a lie and my body and my mind are paying the price."

"Well, you may change your mind before the twenty-fifth."

"No, I won't. I have to get out before I completely — break down."

Somewhat relieved, I started to let my hair grow then. Although I had offered to complete the academic year for the sake of the students, on the Saturday before Easter I was whisked away like the others had been, early in the morning. Forbidden contact with anyone, for two days I was sequestered in a private room of St. Vincent's Hospital.

"Thank God I'm not a patient here," I thought as I lay in bed the night before my departure. "At least I'm getting out. I wonder how many nuns are in this hospital who will never get out."

Fifty pounds lighter than when I had entered ten years before and dressed in a plain suit, I boarded the plane for California. The community gave me $300 in cash to start a new life.

I had failed at the greatest undertaking of my life. My search for God and fulfillment had ended in disillusionment and despair — another steel door closed.

8

A Burnt-Out Shell

Where can I go from Thy Spirit?
Or where can I flee from Thy presence?
If I ascend to heaven, Thou art there;
If I make my bed in Sheol, behold,
Thou art there.
If I take the winds of the dawn,
If I dwell in the remotest part of the sea.
Even there Thy hand will lead me,
And Thy right hand will lay hold of me.
(Ps. 139:7-10)

The one person in the whole world whom I really wanted to see again would not be there when I stepped off the plane in California.

I had been in Iowa a year when, one evening just before dinner, the Sister Superior told me I had a phone call from my mother. I knew it must have been very important because my mother seldom called. My parents had only visited me once, when they were returning from a wedding in New England.

"Mother, what is it?"

"Your grandmother died very early this morning."

"What — what happened?"

"She just sat up in bed and had a brief spell of nausea and then she expired."

"Did — did she suffer?"

"No, no pain. She was mentally bright and in good spirits, right until the last. They won't let you come for the funeral, will they?"

"No, it isn't allowed...." To myself, I thought, "What good would it do now, anyway?" How I would have loved to have seen her before she went.

"Mother," I continued, "like dad, I've never been much for funerals anyway. It seems like an awful lot of fuss over an empty cocoon after the butterfly has flown away."

I don't remember the rest of the conversation. I held everything in through evening prayers. Weeping softly into my pillow that night, I cried, "O God, please let me see my Nama again someday — "

Dreading the idea of meeting my parents at the airport and having to admit my failure, I tried to keep my thoughts elsewhere.

My mind rushed back to the time when, in late 1959, Pope John XXIII had announced that he was going to convene a Second Vatican Council for the specific purpose of "updating" the Catholic Church. During the early sixties we heard numerous reports of progressive communities beginning to follow the trend of modernization. Ours was more conservative and basically resistant to reform.

The only significant change that was introduced while I was still a member was the modification of the habit. In September, 1964, following the mandate of Rome, a simplified, streamlined habit was introduced. Instead of spending two hours every Saturday starching our headpieces and collars on large tins, we were free to use our time planning lessons and correcting papers. Most of us were very grateful for the new, easy-care clothing. We didn't always express our feelings for fear of offending the older nuns, many of whom were attached to the traditional habit.

Although I didn't realize it at the time, I was in the vanguard of what would be many thousands of nuns and priests who would leave their orders during the sixties and seventies.

After I had returned to California, I would occasionally receive a phone call or letter apprising me of some other sister's departure from the community.

The attractive, devout Sister Kelly had been sent to a distant land as a missionary. There she fell in love with and eventually married a Maryknoll priest.

Another young sister renowned for her piety had encountered a situation similar to mine. She was a highly competent nurse and many of the older sisters were jealous of her abilities and accomplishments. They had systematically shunned her. One evening, as they were all seated for dinner, she asked three different sisters to pass the butter. After the third one deliberately ignored her, she stood, swore at them, grabbed a large platter of spaghetti and hurled it the entire length of the table. She then walked out the front door of the hospital and never returned.

Sister J., a beautiful, loving, kindergarten teacher, ended up in a convent where the Superior had a "special friend." These two, powerful matriarchs did not even try to conceal their feelings toward her. They openly and deliberately made life miserable for her.

At 3:00 one afternoon, Sister J. dismissed her class, told them to always remember that she loved them, picked up one paper bag and walked downtown. She went to a pay phone and called her parents. Saying only, "Do not tell anyone else. I'm at the corner of Fifth and Adams. I will wait here for you," she stood in that spot until her panicked parents picked her up nine hours later.

Sister R., who had been admonished by Sister Bernadette for playing "footsie" behind the door, obtained a high-paying position after she left the convent, but she never found peace. Her body was discovered one day, with a loaded revolver still in her hand.

The list is endless.

It is all quite different now. The nuns are given much more freedom; the rule of silence has been relaxed; they are allowed to eat with their families and others; most of them are permitted to swim and engage in other athletic activities; they are free to travel; many live in cheerfully decorated homes, instead of austere dormitories; they have discarded medieval garments in favor of regular clothes. Their ranks remain extremely decimated however — a cause of great consternation for the world-wide Roman Catholic Church.

It has been only during the past decade that many religious communities have openly acknowledged the high incidence of mental breakdowns and psychogenic disorders among their members.

What had happened to those of us who had entered with such high ideals and expectations? Was our disintegration a result of our constantly forcing ourselves to achieve the impossible?

"Would you care for a cocktail?" Turning from the window, it took me a few seconds to realize the flight attendant was addressing me.

"Sure, why not?" I thought to myself. Nodding intently as she listed the various drinks, I repeated the name of one that sounded the most sophisticated. I don't remember exactly what it was, but the effects were immediate. My head was still swimming when she set the tray of food before me an hour later. It was then that I first noticed that the young man in the aisle seat was smiling at me.

"You didn't eat much. Does flying make you nervous?"

"No, not really. It's just that I haven't been home for a long time." I left it at that.

He seemed to want to talk, so I just listened, wondering whether I should look directly at him. I remembered then that as I was boarding, he had politely stood to let me get into my seat. In passing, my arm had brushed against his and I had immediately jerked back, saying, "Oh, I'm sorry." For many months, it would be my automatic response to anyone's touching me. After years of suppression, I had to retrain my body to become an expression of myself.

As I entered Los Angeles International Airport, there didn't seem to be anyone waiting to greet me. As I scanned the crowd, I saw my parents still looking toward the plane. I had walked right past them and they hadn't recognized me. Coming up behind them, I said, "I'm here."

Startled, my mother replied, "Patricia, you — you look so different. You've lost weight. Well, that's good...." She never asked about the circumstances causing the weight loss, and I never volunteered any information. It would be years before I could ever speak to anyone about what I had undergone in the convent.

I lived with my sister and her family for a while, but I wanted to be independent as soon as possible. I rented a small studio apartment near California State University, where I attended graduate classes in the evening. I taught at a large Catholic high school and then in a public school after I received my California credentials.

When people want to illustrate the rapid but imperceptible decline of morals in our country (frog-in the-pot-of-water scenario), they often use the example of the missionary being in the jungle of South America for five years, then returning to our civilization. I can certainly attest to that assessment. I came back to a world which had turned upside-down. Things which we had been brought up to cherish — respect for God, the family, country, order, morality — were now held in contempt. For me, this was first-degree culture shock.

Because I did not want to be considered "odd," I fearfully guarded my past. I wore the latest fashions and hairdos so that I wouldn't bear the faintest resemblance to an ex-nun. When I would be at a party and someone started asking leading questions —wondering why I lived alone, was still single, had never married — I would deftly turn the conversation to another subject. Existentialism was the rage then, so I would begin talking about Sartre or Camus. The bland serenity that I had practiced so long came in handy.

Although many people around me smoked pot or took other drugs, I never tried them. I did drink alcohol at social gatherings. With a cigarette and drink in hand, I struck the pose of the pensive, detached intellectual. I did not know then what I am now convinced of: both alcohol and nicotine are very dangerous, addictive drugs.

I still went to Mass on Sundays and on holy days of obligation and received the sacraments, but it was without my former zeal. Religion was part of my background and tradition, but I would never again pour my life out for it. I couldn't risk any more pain.

One day I saw an ad in the newspaper in which a sports publication sought a proofreader/copywriter. Since I thought it would be a good way to earn extra money on a part-time basis, I applied and got the job. All the people in the office were really amiable and I enjoyed working with them. Although our initial encounter was tense — "Who is this Pat Nolan who red pencils all over my articles?" — the owner, Peter Savas, and I became friends.

Unlike other men who sent me flowers and took me

to fancy restaurants and fed me "lines," Peter was absolutely straightforward. He had given up drinking years before. He wasn't too fond of parties or social gatherings. Although he had a law degree, he was unpretentious. He liked hot dogs, baseball and fishing.

After I had worked there for about six months, Peter took me out for coffee one afternoon. I told him about my background, my insecurities, why I felt fragmented and not ready for any serious relationship. When I finished, he just looked at me and said, "You are going to marry me someday."

"Oh, really?" I replied. "What makes you think so?"

"Because — well, we just belong together, you know — like — like a pair of old shoes."

I laughed so hard that everyone in the coffee shop turned to look at us.

"What's so funny?"

"Well, that's just the most unromantic thing I've ever heard in my entire life."

His sincerity touched me. Somehow I knew that I could trust this man with my life. He would accept me just the way I was. He would protect me. He would always be there for me.

For over a year, I wrestled with the decision to marry Peter. Because he had been married before, I knew that I would be ex-communicated from the sacramental life of the church and be in a state of mortal sin until the annulment came through from Rome. According to Canon Law, I knew that he had valid grounds for an annulment, but I also knew that the process was very involved and expensive. It would require five to ten years to clear the bureaucracy of the Roman Rota. (By the time the permission was granted, seven years later, we were already "very married.")

Another deep dilemma was the responsibility of marrying a man with four children whose emotional needs were considerable. They were all girls under the age of twelve.

I received no encouragement from friends. They all tried to dissuade me from marrying a man with such burdens when there were other prospects available who were "free."

Also, I had planned to have three children of my own and it was heartrending for me to give up that hope. I went away to a monastery in the high desert to pray about it for several days.

One afternoon I was sitting alone, agonizing over this decision, when a thought came vividly to my mind. In Catholic school, we would collect money every day for the missions to save the "pagan babies." Over the top of the chart in the classroom which indicated how much money we had sent to the missionaries was the Scripture, " *Whoever receives one such child in my name receives Me.*" (Matt. 18:5). I strongly sensed then that, even though it was contrary to church law, I was to marry this man and take his children. It wasn't in the form of a command; it was more along the lines of, "Will you?"

I got on my knees and in the midst of grieving for my own dead dreams, I said aloud, "I receive these children in your name, Jesus."

Peter and I were married in a private civil ceremony and within a year I had five children —Marika, Kiki, Christina, Katie and our son, Joseph.

What I learned about stepparenting, mostly through trial and error, would fill pages. It was extremely difficult at times. I made a lot of mistakes but I always asked the Lord to make up for my failings. All of our children are dedicated Christians today, for which I give God all the glory. I love them very much and I would not trade them for anyone. (I hope they wouldn't trade me.) Recently one of my daughters said, "Mom, I think you got to do your social work with us." We were able to laugh together at the Lord's sense of humor. We are family.

Every Sunday, Peter and I would take the children to Mass. When it came time for the communion, I would watch the others file up to the railing while I sat in the pew. I tried very hard not to show my deep distress at not being able to participate. Sometimes the tears would roll down my cheeks and the children would ask, "Mom, what's wrong?"

"Nothing, it's nothing. You go ahead up." Looking longingly at the tabernacle I would pray, "Lord, they tell me that you don't love me anymore, but I still love you."

Often at night I couldn't sleep. When I did, I would have terrible nightmares. I would wake up screaming and trembling. One night Peter put his arms around me and asked, "What is it? What keeps terrifying you like this?"

"God is angry with me because I married outside the church. He's going to send me to hell."

Peter, who was brought up in a Greek Orthodox home and had a lot more common sense than I did, tried to reassure me. "Listen. That's a bunch of nonsense. If I love you as much as any human being could ever love —and I do — just think how much more God loves you."

I appreciated his devotion, but it didn't assuage the terror in my soul.

When I was eight months pregnant with Joseph, I remember how we came within inches of a fatal car collision. The last thought that flashed across my mind was, "God, please don't punish this baby, too."

The migraines which had plagued me for years intensified as I tried to play the multiple roles of perfect wife, perfect mother, perfect teacher. Although no one was aware of it, I was on constant medication for the headaches. From the exterior, I looked as though I had it all together. Inside, however, I was dying.

I decided to sign up for a college course which I thought would be beneficial to me in the future. (I've never really used it.) It was there that I met a woman named Yolanda Wallace. Through my association with this beautiful, gentle person, my life would be changed forever.

9

From Ashes to Beauty

The Spirit of the Lord God is upon me,
because the Lord has anointed me to bring
good news to the afflicted; He has sent me to
bind up the brokenhearted,
To proclaim liberty to captives, and freedom
to prisoners;
To proclaim the favorable year of the Lord,
And the day of vengeance of our God:
To comfort all who mourn,
To grant those who mourn in Zion,
Giving them a garland instead of ashes,
The oil of gladness instead of mourning,
The mantle of praise instead of a spirit of
fainting.
So they will be called oaks of righteousness,
The planting of the Lord, that He may be
glorified.

(Isa. 61:1-3)

During class breaks, Yolanda and I would carry on casual discussions. She was originally from Bogota, Colombia, and had married an American seventeen years before. She had lived in the United States ever since. As I began to trust this kind woman, I revealed my background to her.

Saying only, "You might be interested in this," Yolanda offered me a book one day. It was entitled *Aglow With the Spirit* by Dr. Robert Frost. I could not put it down, and I read it until dawn. (It remains among the top ten anointed books that changed my life.) One by one, she fed me other books, all of which were written by contemporaries whose lives had been radically changed by their personal encounters with Christ and subsequent filling with His Holy Spirit. I devoured them all. Deep within the murky tomb of my spirit I felt the faintest stirrings of — could it possibly be — hope?

After class one day, Yolanda asked me, "Would you like to go to a prayer meeting with me some Tuesday evening?"

"Well, I don't think I can — I've never been to anything like that outside the Catholic church. We're not allowed."

Cheerfully she broke in, "Oh, it's not in a church building or anything like that — just some people gathered in a home. By the way, many of them are Catholics."

"Really? Sure I'd love to go."

The first thing that I noticed about those twenty-eight people sitting around the living room of that modest home in Ocean Beach was their joy. It wasn't the rehearsed "cheerfulness" that I had been accustomed to; it was a genuine openness and warmth that seemed to bubble up from an inner source.

The next thing that impressed me was the profound sincerity of their worship. When they prayed, it wasn't with the distanced sense of "Thee and Thou." They were talking to a God whom they knew well and He, apparently, was hearing and answering. As they went from singing simple, moving songs in English to singing in the Spirit, I was so awestruck that I just sat in a corner and quietly cried. "This is as close to any angelic choir that I'm going to get on this earth," I thought.

The God in that little room was *real* and *alive* — not the God of stained glass and marble, of incense and rote chants. He was the God of the living!

After that, I lived for Tuesday evenings. In between, I'd pray, "God, I know that I'm a rotten sinner, I know that the church says I'm going to hell, but — if only, if only, I could just touch you, could know you, like those people in Ocean Beach. If only I knew that you loved me — "

For the next two prayer meetings, I continued to sit in a corner just absorbed in the wonder of it all. Then an urgency began to overtake me. Like the woman in the gospel who had suffered with a hemorrhage of blood for twelve years, I was dying and life was "out there." A tremendous surge of boldness welled up within me. I had to press through the suffocating throng of uncertainties, anxieties, apprehensions. *I had to, I had to touch* the hem of His garment!

Before the fourth meeting, I had said a simple prayer in my heart, "Lord, you know my heart. If this is for me, let someone come to me and say it."

At the break, one of the leaders approached me. "I've been praying for you. The Lord told me that you want to be prayed for. Do you understand the baptism in the Holy Spirit?"

"Yes." (Thanks to Yolanda's preparing me with the books.)

"Well, we will lay hands on you as witnesses, but it is Jesus himself who immerses you in His Spirit. You must ask Him and He *will* do it if you ask, as He says in Luke 11:13. Do you understand?"

"Yes."

He led me in a simple prayer, acknowledging that I was a sinner, that Jesus had saved me by His death on the cross and that I wanted Him to be Lord of my life. Then I humbly asked Him to baptize me in His Holy Spirit. While the others continued to pray, I silently pleaded, "O my God, my God, if only I knew that you loved me, I could make it. Otherwise, I'm not going to. Just let me know that you love me." Something so remarkable then transpired that it almost seems beyond verbal explanation. I actually felt a heavy weight lift. It started at my toes — a dark burden of sin, guilt, despair, doubt and fear. It kept rising — past my knees, my hips, my waist. As it lifted from my chest and upward, something in my heart exploded like a geyser that had been uncapped. Living waters gushed forth and with them a heavenly language! As an awesome peace enveloped me, the Father's voice resounded, "*I have loved you with an everlasting love; Therefore I have drawn you with lovingkind-*

ness" (Jer. 31:3). It was followed by, *"Never be bound by man's rules again."*

I had been *set free!*

Within the finite limits of semantics, how can one ever describe the split-second movement of a soul from darkness to light, from death to life? Jesus said, *"No man can come unto Me, unless the Father who sent me draws him; and I will raise him up on the last day"* (John 6:44).

That is exactly what happened. The Father, in His infinite mercy, had apprehended me in grace and brought me to His Son.

It was then that I began to *know* Jesus as a Person. If I thought that writing the next statement in my blood would free someone from deception, I would willingly do it: There is a universe of difference between knowing *about* Jesus and *knowing* Jesus.

To those of you who tell me how religious you are, how many times you attend church, how many prayers you repeat, how many good works you do, how many degrees you have in theology, I answer, "But have you *met* the *man*?"

From that moment years ago until the present I have been through many personal tribulations, through dark nights of the soul, through wilderness wanderings, through physical illness and through family problems. But, there has never been an instant since that November night in 1970 when I haven't said, "You and I, Jesus, we're going to make it — somehow, we're going to make it."

With the Apostle Paul, I exclaim:

*Who shall separate us from the love of Christ?
Shall tribulation, or distress, or persecution, or
famine, or nakedness, or peril, or sword?
Just as it is written, "For Thy sake we are being put to death all day long; We were considered as sheep to be slaughtered."
But in all these things we overwhelmingly con-
quer through Him who loved us.
For I am convinced that neither death, nor life,
nor angels, nor principalities, nor things present,
nor things to come, nor powers, nor height, nor
depth, nor any other created thing, shall be able
to separate us from the love of God, which is in
Christ Jesus our Lord.*

(Rom. 8:35-39)

I had noticed that almost all of the persons who attended the prayer meetings carried Bibles. Sometimes
they would read aloud to the group from a passage
which they felt was particularly significant. I purchased
a Bible in a Catholic bookstore. It was *The Jerusalem Bible*, an excellent translation. (It is regrettable that more
Catholics don't read it.) One of the first things I noted in
2 Timothy 3:16 was, *"All Scripture is inspired by God...."*

"All Scripture?" I marveled, *"All* inspired by God?"

Then why didn't someone hand me this book years
ago and say, "Here is the God-breathed owner's manu-
al for your life?" Whenever I would ponder this question, I was affected by an inner dissatisfaction that I
couldn't define.

Besides having the Scriptures come alive with meaning, another immediate result of my personal encounter with Jesus and His immersing me in His Holy Spirit was the spiritual *power* I experienced in my life. The Lord says in Acts 1:8: *"But you shall receive power when the Holy Spirit has come upon you; and you shall be My witnesses both in Jerusalem, and in all Judea and Samaria, and even to the remotest part of the earth."*

Before, I had wanted to do right, but I lacked the prevailing grace or strength to overcome. Now I was emboldened with a strong, spiritual vitality — in prayer, in sharing the gospel, in conquering sinful desires and choosing good, in handling the ordinary vicissitudes of everyday life.

It was an enormous relief to know that my entering the presence of the Father was not dependent on religious practices or personal worth — neither my own nor anyone else's. It was solely through the blood of the Lamb that I was enabled to approach the throne. God's Word assured me:

> *Therefore, He [Jesus] had to be made like His brethren in all things, that He might become a merciful and faithful high priest in things pertaining to God, to make propitiation for the sins of the people;* (Heb. 2:17)

and,

> *Hence, also, He is able to save forever those who draw near to God through Him, since He always lives to make intercession for them;* (Heb. 7:25)

117

The assurance that my blessed Savior is constantly before the Father interceding for me was and is one of the greatest comforts of my life. To even hint that any other mediator is needed, or indeed even possible, is to deny the almighty power of the precious blood and the divinity of the One who shed it.

My joyful metamorphosis was apparent. Marika asked if she could accompany me to the prayer meetings. After she likewise changed, Peter had two "spiritual butterflies" to contend with. We never pressed him, but the curiosity was too much for him. He offered to go with us one evening saying only, "I'm going to sit by the door. If anything 'funny' goes on, I'm leaving." He kept going back. Months later the Lord Jesus would make himself real to Peter also.

I met a priest at one of these meetings who, as we were leaving, posed the rhetorical question, "Why have we been preaching pie-in-the-sky-when-you-die all these years when we should be telling people they can have eternal life *now*, joy *now*, peace *now*?"

Good question. I hope he found the answer. I never saw him after that night.

We were hoping to purchase a particular house in Vista which we really liked a lot, but the prospects looked doubtful. Peter and I prayed about it and we promised the Lord that we would open it up one evening a week for prayer meetings if the escrow passed; it did and we were delighted.

After we had been there two days, a woman approached the house holding out a loaf of homemade banana bread. "Hi, I'm Cathie Grove, one of your neighbors." I introduced myself. She then asked, "Are you a Christian?"

I gave her a quizzical look, "Yes."

"Oh, I knew it! Praise God! From the time that 'For Sale' sign went up, I've been praying for someone like you to move in!" We formed a lasting friendship.

Keeping our promise to God, we opened our house for weekly prayer meetings to whomever He sent. That first week it was just our family, Cathie and her best friend, Elaine White.

Within a month the meeting grew to twenty people, then thirty — men, women and children. They were from various backgrounds — Baptist, Catholic, Pentecostal, Seventh Day Adventist, Lutheran, Episcopalian, etc. Some had no past denominational affiliations. It was very similar to the early Christians — one would come with a song; another with a Scripture; several with testimonies; many with prayer requests.

Although we have long since gone our separate ways, whenever I meet these people, they invariably remark that it was the purest worship and praise they've ever known. Perhaps it was because no one was trying to teach any particular doctrines or sign people up for their denominations or push their pet dogmas. They shared only one common purpose — to lift up Jesus the Messiah in prayer and praise.

After I read in the Bible, *"But the Helper, the Holy Spirit, whom the Father will send in My name, He will teach you all things, and bring to your remembrance all that I said to you"* (John 14:26), I knelt down by the side of my bed. Placing my left hand on the Scripture, I prayed, "Now, Lord, you said here that you would send me the Holy Spirit, which you've done. Thank you. You also said that He would teach me whatever was necessary. I'm trusting in your Word here to do just that. I am just a dumb sheep — woolly-faced and often woolly-brained, and I really need your constant guidance. I'm asking you please to put your hand heavily right here (I grabbed the top of my head with my right hand) and do not let go of me — no matter what. Amen."

From that moment, He became my Teacher and Counselor. A phenomenal thing happened. One day I could have filled several blue examination booklets with Aquinas's proofs for the existence of God, the next day I couldn't remember even one theological treatise. I had become a *tabula rasa* — a clean slate, and God himself would begin to write on me, one simple stroke at a time.

10

The Healing Balm of Forgiveness

"If you love Me, you will keep My commandments. And I will ask the Father, and He will give you another Helper, that He may be with you forever; that is the Spirit of truth . . . ."

John 14:15-17

A word of explanation may be in order before you read the next section. I will be speaking of hearing God's voice. It is difficult to describe this experience adequately. The sound doesn't come from within or without, but both — as if the entire being is a bell and the message reverberates throughout.

Please do not think I am some kind of visionary or mystic. I'm not. I'm just a sinner saved by grace. Over the past twenty-one years, this phenomenon has occurred fewer than five times, primarily at the beginning of my Christian walk. Maybe it was because I was so entrenched in religious beliefs and confused by the teachings of men.

God speaks to us daily in many ways, usually in a "still, small voice." Sometimes He'll speak through the reading of the Word or through a set of circumstances. Often He'll send the same message through several totally unrelated sources, and it will be a confirmation of something we've been praying about. It is imperative to check every impression we may have received against the written Word of God. There are a lot of strange "voices" in the world, especially in this era of New Age deception.

We are commanded: *"Beloved, do not believe every spirit, but test the spirits to see whether they are from God; because many false prophets have gone out into the world"* (1 John 4:1).

Approximately six months after we had moved into our house in Vista, I was deep in worship during the prayer meeting, concentrating on the wonders of the Savior. Clearly, in a voice filled with inexplicable love, He said: *"This is my Church."* It was so unexpected that I drew in my breath sharply as I lifted my head to gaze around the room. This group of various backgrounds, denominations, educations, jobs — this very ordinary gathering of ordinary people — was the true Church. What a revelation that was to me!

It is one thing to read on paper that the original meaning of the Church is derived from *ekklesia* (Greek for "called out"), and quite another to experience it.

Ever since that moment, I have been very conscious of the fact that the Body of Messiah, the true Church, comprises living cells, people — not buildings, rituals, programs, hierarchies, tenets. Whenever I am praying with another believer, whether it be at the beach or under a tree or in a room — I always remember, *"This is my Church."*

Then, without audible words, but just as clearly, God began to make known to me the fact that He was delivering me from spirits of religiosity. As my life passed before me, what petrified me was the knowledge that I had to give up my *security.*

At that moment I felt as though I was being tossed about on a vast, tumultuous, black ocean. Frantically I had clung to one little lifesaver, religion. Now God was asking me to let go of that buoy, to reach out into the darkness and in faith believe that He would grasp my hand. Mourning as a large part of me fell into that churning sea, I stretched forth my right hand and simply said, "Yes."

Although I did not fully understand it at the time, that evening marked my initial passage from religion to relationship.

Months later, I read in Genesis 12:1:

> *Now the Lord said to Abram, "Go forth from your country, and from your relatives and from your father's house, to the land which I will show you...."*

I commiserated with that great patriarch who simply believed God and *"went out, not knowing where he was going..."* (Heb. 11:8) .

I had wondered a long time about the role which the saints played in our Christian walk. How were we to regard those examples of holiness who had gone on before us? One day I prayed, "Father, I ask you, in Jesus' name, to please show me the truth about this." I let the matter go to a "back burner," trusting that He would answer my request in His own perfect time and way.

Months later, a family member was totally absorbed in a movie, *The Song of Bernadette,* on T.V. Something was bothering me about it, but I didn't know exactly what. Then the Father spoke: *"Anything that takes your eyes off my Son, no matter how good it appears, is not of me."*

That was it -- simple, direct, uncomplicated. The Word of God later confirmed that "*Even Satan disguises himself as an angel of light*" (2 Cor. 11:14). Another passage gave me a clear answer: "*For there is one God, and* one mediator *also between God and men, the man Christ Jesus* (1 Tim. 2:15, emphasis mine).

The mother of Jesus deserves the same consideration and respect as the other disciples. She certainly was the first. I often think that she and John, as well as Mary Magdalene, underwent their respective martyrdoms at the foot of the cross. They all loved Jesus intensely and it must have caused them immense agony to stay there and watch Him suffer and die. She truly did endure a sword piercing her heart. She was, however, completely human and not divine, which totally disqualifies her as a "mediatrix" or bridge between God and us. Jesus himself put it all in correct perspective when He said:

---

* "execution stake," in Hebrew.

"For whoever does the will of God, he is My brother and sister and mother" (Mark 3:35).

Although the suffering of the mother of Jesus is widely acknowledged, how many of us have ever meditated on what it cost the Father to stand by and watch His only begotten Son bear the rage of demons and the ravages of men? This was the absolutely sinless Lamb — the heart of His very heart — who had been in perfect oneness with Him since before time began, in a union of love which we cannot begin to comprehend.

Perhaps a woman who has had her womb and heart torn from her in the loss of an only child can have some appreciation of the pain. The rest of us can't even begin to empathize.

"For God so loved the world. . ." (John 3:16).

When we are first enjoying the milk of the believer's delight in our newly found relationship with Christ, everything usually goes blissfully well. All our prayers seem to be answered, we move through an exhilarating succession of small and large miracles. Life becomes an exciting, spiritual adventure.

As the Lord began to wean me from the milk and lead me into the meat of the gospel (see Hebrews 5:12-14), He presented me with the inescapable, absolute qualifications for discipleship:

> *Then Jesus said to His disciples, "If anyone wishes to come after Me, let him deny himself, and take up his cross* and follow Me. For whoever wishes to save his life shall lose it; but whoever loses his life for My sake shall find it."*
> *(Matt. 16:24-25)*

125

It was at this point, He taught me the supreme importance of forgiveness. I went through a period when I felt as though my prayers were hitting the ceiling and bouncing back. I mentioned this to an older, saintly woman and she quickly responded, "Is there anyone whom you haven't forgiven? There are many stumbling blocks to spiritual progress, but unforgiveness is the greatest. If someone comes to your mind, you must forgive them immediately. Do not let the sun go down another day before you have asked Jesus to help you forgive. If you can't see that person soon, then at least make the intention — say it right out loud — and as soon as you get an opportunity, make it right with them."

As I thanked her and turned to leave, she cautioned me, "There are *no conditions* attached to forgiveness. You never, ever try to change that person. You never hope to have them recognize their mistakes or tell you that they are sorry. You leave all of that up to God. You forgive for only one reason — it is the clear, unqualified injunction of your Lord and Savior:

> *"For if you forgive men for their transgressions,*
> *your heavenly Father will also forgive you. But*
> *if you do not forgive men, then your Father will*
> *not forgive your transgressions."*
>
> *(Matt. 6:14-15)*

When I left that woman's house, I knew what the Lord required of me, but I did not want to face it. I also realized that unless I obeyed, never again would I be able to pray, "...*and forgive us our debts as* (to the same degree) *we forgive our debtors...* " without calling judgment down on myself.

126

That evening, as I was alone in my room, the pervading peace and joy which had been my portion since that night in Ocean Beach gave way to a mounting anxiety, "I can't, Lord — I just can't!" But I knew that I had to. An immense struggle ensued.

By this time, I was down on my knees, face in hands, "O Jesus, help me!" By opening myself to forgiveness, I also knew that I was unlocking the floodgates to all the excruciatingly painful memories of my childhood. "Mother, I — I — " A stifling, agonizing vise gripped my throat — I couldn't get the words out. Then a thought impressed itself strongly on my mind, "Look to the cross."

I found myself at the foot of the cross, gazing at my beloved Savior, beaten and tortured beyond recognition. He seemed to say, *"Father, forgive them for they know not what they are doing...."*

I realized that it was only through the cross that I would be able to do this. Keeping the eyes of my mind fixed steadily on Him, I said, "This is for you, Jesus. I lay it on your cross: 'Mother, I forgive you, in Jesus' name.'"

I lost all track of time as gigantic sobs racked my body and streams of anger and anguish gushed out. I came to myself much later. I was lying prostrate on the floor, my head resting on my arms. Tranquility had returned.

As I drove to visit my mother, I reflected, "Well, now, how does a person really say this, without causing more hurt? I can't very well say, 'I forgive you for being a terrible mother.' You'll have to help me, Lord."

I knew she was even more angry with me since I'd married a divorced man, even though Peter had done the honorable thing in announcing his intentions to both of my parents before we married. As the emotional temperature in the room rose, my mother sat through the entire evening just glaring at me. The only remark she made was, "Patricia is very naïve, you know. She hasn't been out of the convent too long, and I don't think she really knows what she wants."

Finally, dad turned to me and said, "Do you want to marry him?"

"Yes."

"Then, I guess that's all that matters."

She had never accepted Peter. Whenever anyone would ask her if it was true that I had married a man with several children, her only comment was, "Out of the convent, into the frying pan."

As I parked in my parents' driveway I whispered, "Help me, Lord."

We talked about ordinary things that afternoon. As the usual verbal jabs flew my way, however, I was now consciously aware of trying not to let them elicit an angry response from me. In my mind, I kept saying, "In Jesus' name, I forgive...," but the opportunity never presented itself to do anything more than that.

As I started to leave, I went over to mother's chair where she was still seated. Taking one of her hands in mine, I kissed her on the forehead and said, "I love you, Mother."

She stiffened, obviously flustered. "Love, love, love. That's all you and your sister's generation ever talk about. What is all this love stuff about, anyway? Didn't

I give you the best of everything? Didn't I send you to the finest schools?"

Previously I would have responded with hurt. Now I just smiled and said, "Yes, you did. Thanks, I appreciate what you did for me. I'll see you soon, okay?"

I would like to be able to say that my relationship with my mother went smoothly from that point on; it didn't. It remained a source of tribulation for me, and the Lord exercised me in both asking for and granting forgiveness numerous times.

As I sat studying the Hebrew names of God one morning, I came across something which caused a true transformation within me.

Most of the Old Testament names for God — *Yahweh, Adonai, El elyon* — are masculine in form. But Genesis 5:1-3 affirms that both male and female are in the image of the Creator, *Elohiym*. Also, *El Shaddai*, which has commonly come to mean "The Almighty" or "The Strong One," was also interpreted by some scholars in its original form as "the many-breasted God." My spirit leaped within me as I realized that my God was, in a very real sense, all the mother and father I would ever need. Just as a mother's milk provides complete nourishment for her child, I could rest on El Shaddai's breast and have *all* of my needs met perfectly.

What a deliverance that was! It no longer mattered what kind of a childhood I had. It wouldn't even have mattered if I had been orphaned. I was free to really let go of the past.

When I began to understand spiritual warfare, I was able to accept my mother just as she was. *"For our strug-*

gle is not against flesh and blood, but against the rulers, against the powers, against the world forces of this darkness..." (Eph. 6:12).

As my spiritual eyes were opened, I began to see this flesh-and-blood person as a prisoner of her own emotions and the dark spirits that tormented her. Child of an abusive, alcoholic father, she was so bound up with unforgiveness herself that she could not express love.

Two years ago I stood by her bed and thanked her again for all that she had done for me. I also asked her forgiveness for any grief I had caused her. Stroking her head, I told her, as I had many times in the past, "I love you, mother."

Gazing up at me from her frail frame, she whispered, "I love you, too." Wonder of all wonders! I never thought that I would hear those words. She died a few weeks later.

Throughout the past two decades I've been the beneficiary of numerous miracles — deliverances and healings of body, soul and spirit — sometimes occurring simultaneously. When I was delivered from the spirit of perfectionism, for example, the migraine headaches went with it.

I count as the single greatest miracle of my life the genuine love which God gave me for my mother. If anyone had told me in my youth that it would ever have been possible, I would have vehemently denied it.

"With men this is impossible, but with God all things are possible" (Matt. 19:26).

I don't know how we Christians can ever be lights in a dark world if we persist in a "poor me" attitude while continuing to place blame on others for all our problems. Until we obey God and allow Him to heal us His way, we will go through life futilely placing "Band-Aids" on deep, festering wounds.

On this battleground of life, we are surrounded by pathetically crippled, mortally afflicted souls who are desperate to witness a power greater than themselves which will completely heal their gaping wounds, from the inside out.

We are all victims of some kind or other, including the people we are blaming for our own hurts. This is the result of our being born into a fallen, sin-laden world.

"The Son of God appeared for this purpose, that He might destroy the works of the devil "(1 John 3:8). Not to take away, not to overcome, but to *destroy* -- that is, to *totally annihilate* every work of the devil — in the world, in others, in us.

If we believe these words, why don't we live them? Either our God is all-powerful or He is not God. If He is, we have to trust that He will work every single thing in our lives for good.

One of the most poignant passages in the Bible was spoken by Joseph in Genesis. Because of jealousy, his ten older brothers stripped him, beat him severely and left him in a very deep pit or cistern to die. (Talk about rejection and abuse!) Can you just imagine this poor seventeen-year-old, weeping and crying out for help? After all, what had he done to deserve this? The brothers decided to sell him instead. While a slave in Egypt, Joseph was falsely accused of rape and put into prison.

Never once did he blame God or others. He just kept trusting in Elohim.

After God rewarded Joseph's faithfulness by raising him to the highest position in Egypt, next to Pharaoh, his brothers were afraid he would use his great power to get revenge. Instead, he turned to them and said:

> *"You meant evil against me, but God meant it for good in order to bring about this present result, to preserve many people alive."*
>
> *(Gen. 50:20)*

Because of Joseph's forgiveness, the entire nation of Israel was saved from famine and destruction. How many people have been "preserved" as a result of our forgiveness?

Rejection in some form or other is at the root of most of our problems. The Lamb of God suffered the ultimate rejection for us on the cross so that we could go there and release ours forever. Only then will be able to say:

> *Forgetting what lies behind*
> *and reaching forward to what lies ahead,*
> *I press on toward the goal*
> *for the prize of the upward call of God*
> *in Christ Jesus.*
>
> *(Phil. 3:13, 14)*

11

Free Indeed

*If therefore the Son shall make you free, you shall
be free indeed.*

(John 8:36)

"Well, what *are* you, anyway?"

It never ceases to amuse me when people approach
me with that question. What is that peculiarity of human nature which always wants to pigeon-hole others
into convenient categories?

My customary response to such a query is: "I am a
believer in Jesus the Messiah, learning to be a disciple,
seeking to become an overcomer." (The exegesis of those
three terms in the New Testament constitutes an enlight-
ening Bible study.)

Recently, after speaking to an interdenominational
group in San Diego, a man approached me. It was obvious that he was in a state of controlled fury. Gleaming

from his eyes was a spirit so full of hate that it actually looked like it wanted to kill me, to silence me forever. I reminded myself that this was no flesh-and-blood battle. As he spoke, I sent up my favorite prayer, on a red flag: "Help!"

"You talk like all those people and incidents in the Scriptures are literal. You obviously haven't kept current with the latest theological studies or you would know that it's mostly apocryphal, that Satan is not a real being, but merely a personification of evil forces."

At that point, I realized I was up against the worst kind of giant, a tower of intellectual pride. The Lord had taught me long ago never to become embroiled in theological debates. They only cause more division in the sorely torn Body of Christ. To prove points, we often use the Bible as a lethal weapon, bludgeoning our opponents instead of holding it as the source of instruction and inspiration that it was meant to be.

As he continued to sputter, and the redness rose above his clerical collar, I reminded the Lord Jesus, as I always do before I speak, that I was only the little "mouse" sent out to give the message, but He was the "elephant" doing all the work. I called upon His grace, to enable me to remain calm, His power to bind the forces of evil and His wisdom to lead me to utter the right words.

"Well," he almost shouted, "you — you — (What? I wondered, "imbecile? ignoramus?"), surely you must have some philosophy — some theology — what is it anyway?"

134

Smiling at him, I finally answered, "Well, since Jesus told us that, unless we become as little children, we would never enter the kingdom, my "theology" has been reduced to four words: *"Stay childlike. Follow Jesus."*

As he stood there, mouth agape, I left to get into my car. All the way home I sang, "I'm so glad Jesus set me free . . . ."

I could not, in good conscience, conclude this book without first making it eminently clear that in no way are these observations intended for any one group. At the risk of appearing redundant, let me again state that religion is a spirit common to all denominations; it doesn't discriminate.

Almost daily I hear statements like, "You know, I was brought up as a _____, but I had no idea what a personal relationship with Jesus Christ even meant until..." In the blank you may place just about every sect within the Protestant, Roman Catholic and Orthodox segments of Christianity.

The Bible is filled with many examples of God's desiring to lead His people into vital relationship and their choosing the sterile confines of religion instead.

As far back as the Exodus of the Israelites from Egypt, this sad fact is apparent. God had released his children from slavery. He had delivered them through the Red Sea and protected and nurtured them in the wilderness. He had borne them on His wings, like a parent eagle and constantly expressed His deep desire for intimacy.

Instead of responding with gratitude, this stiff-necked people went to Moses and said, *"Speak to us your-*

self and we will listen; but let not God speak to us, lest we die."
(Ex. 20:19).

They chose to set up a religious system with Moses as the intermediary rather than to personally respond to their Father God.

Jesus once selected three disciples to go apart with Him up to a high mountain. There He would reveal to them something absolutely thrilling and life-changing. He would give them a vision of the coming Kingdom —to encourage and inspire them, to set their sights toward the future, to give them hope. These privileged three would behold what no human being had ever witnessed — the Messiah and the fulfillment of the Law (Moses) and the Prophets (Elijah) transfigured before them. *"And His face shone like the sun, and His garments became white as light"* (Matt. 17:2). He seemed to be telling them to be of good cheer, never stop growing, keep pressing on. He had something awesome planned for them in the future.

What was Peter's response? *". . . I will make three tabernacles here, one for you, one for Moses, and one for Elijah"* (Matt. 17:4). Isn't that just like us? God wants to move us on to something magnificent, augmenting, dynamic —and what do we want to do? Why, stay right here and build something, of course — a memorial, a system of traditions, a set of doctrines, an organization. Ultimately, we end up constructing a denomination, a glorified box of sorts. It makes us feel secure. It also boxes others out and us in.

So how did that sly spirit, Religion, seduce so many of us? Probably because it's the most innocent-looking and surreptitious of all deceptions.

Persons like me who were very insecure children, always feeling a tremendous need for acceptance and approval, often become addicted to religion the way some people do to alcohol or other drugs. We feel that without it, we just can't cope and our world might fall apart. We are usually even more deceived than other addicts. They at least have some inkling that what they're doing is harmful; we often feel that what we're doing is right, earning some kind of "points" with God and men.

Can a person function within a system, but not be "religious"? Yes, but we have to learn to recognize that counterfeit:

Religion is "I have to."
Relationship is "I want to."

Religion is the parable for the world to read.
Relationship speaks plainly to the listening, watchful
    heart.

Religion requires outward signs or symbols.
Relationship offers, "Come, let me introduce you to the
    living reality behind those symbols."

Religion lifts up certain persons as being better or
    closer to God because of their office, education or
    background.
Relationship recognizes only one Head on the Body of
    Messiah and all the rest as equally important mem
    bers.

Religion sets aside specific days, ceremonies, places, prayers for worship.
Relationship worships the Father in spirit and in truth — anytime, anywhere.

Religion presents an outer form of godliness.
Relationship opens us up for the Lord to enter in and make us a clean vessel to contain Him.

Religion is an obligation, often resulting in guilt and anxiety.
Relationship is an adventure, producing joy and wonder.

Religion attempts to unite people by having them assent to the same doctrines.
Relationship recognizes that only the Spirit of God makes us truly one.

Religion is the schoolteacher, telling about God.
Relationship is experiencing God.

Religion is the letter of the Law of God, which kills and puts us into bondage.
Relationship is the spirit of the Law of God, which gives us life and sets us free.

Religion does things for God.
Relationship abides in God.

Religion is the shadow or blueprint of the real thing.
Relationship is the real thing.

* * * * * * * * * *

God's idea of what religion should be, instead of what man has made it, is found in the Epistle of James 1:27:

> *This is pure and undefiled religion in the sight of our God and Father, to visit orphans and widows in their distress, and to keep oneself unstained by the world.*

John Wesley once cautioned that there is no such thing as a solitary Christian. If we are really attached to each other in the Body of Christ, we must function as one organism. I'm certainly not advocating throwing out the "baby" (fellowship with other Christians) with the "bath water" (vain religious practices).

That we are to assemble with other believers on a regular basis is a clear requirement of God's Word. *"Not forsaking our own assembling together . . . and all the more, as you see the day drawing near"* (Heb. 10:25).

We live in perilous times, growing ever darker each day. Spiritual survival demands that Christians bond together to support, encourage and help each other. If you have not yet found such a vital body of true believers, keep praying, keep searching. They are out there. We need each other.

I have found that if we sincerely seek after truth because we want to know God better in order to love and serve Him more and not merely to appear "learned," He will always reveal it to us. Truth, after all, is a Person: *"Jesus said to him, I am the way, and the truth, and the life ..."* (John 14:6).

139

The Lord always blesses the sincerely searching heart.

An anointed young musician and prophet, Keith Green, once wrote a song that annoyed some churchgoers. (True prophets — those who speak for God — seem to have a knack for upsetting people.) It went, in part:

To obey is better than sacrifice,
I want more than Sundays
And Wednesday nights.
'Cause if you can't come
To Me everyday,
Then don't bother coming at all.**

Of the many things which the Lord has taught me over the past two decades, the foremost is the fact that He is, above all else, a very personal being. He already owns everything in the universe, so there is no material gift that we can give which will please Him. The one thing that he does want and which brings Him great joy when it is freely given, is our heart — not in words only, but in truth and in deed.

Because God is a person, He feels, thinks, knows, grieves and loves in a personal manner. The only way we ever get to really know another person is by communication. That is how God expresses himself to us and

---

**From the song, "To Obey is Better Than Sacrifice" as quoted in *No Compromise: The Life Story of Keith Green* by Melody Green. Copyright 1990 by Sparrow Press, California division of the Sparrow Corp, Nashville, TN. All rights reserved. Reprinted by special permission.

how He wants us to approach Him. Hopefully, this communication will develop into deep communion.

Defenders of sectarianism would have us believe that the organizations themselves produce sanctity. We only have to examine the lives of the proven men and women of God to know that this is not the case.

From Francis of Assisi down to the saints of our era —George Mueller, David Brainerd, Amy Carmichael, A.W. Tozer, Charles Finney, Corrie Ten Boom, Mother Teresa of Calcutta — to name only several of hundreds, it is clear that their personal holiness was not necessarily the direct result of religious affiliation. They were, in fact, often misunderstood by those within the structures.

Radiantly weaving throughout the diverse lives of all of God's faithful ones is a single golden thread: an intimate, passionate, all-consuming love of Jesus Christ.

The Lord has always had His holy remnant. He still has them today — in and out of every denomination — from the streets of New York to the jungles of Honduras. There are probably thousands of them, but we won't even know most of their names until the Messiah comes again to establish His kingdom. Then they will shine as the stars in the firmament for all eternity.

We stand in awe of such total dedication. But isn't this what we are all supposed to be doing — loving God with our whole heart, mind, soul and strength, and loving our neighbors as ourselves; being lights in a dark world, illuminating our little patch of earth and pointing the way toward the Father? Shouldn't this be the normal rather than the supernormal Christian life?

It would require another 200 pages to describe all the learning and unlearning I have undergone over the past twenty-two years. The Master Teacher has been marvelously patient with me. Step by hesitant step, He's still bringing me along the path of righteousness.

I sincerely hope you're convinced of at least one thing, dear reader: Religion cannot save you. You can be, as I was, the most "religious" person in the world and still be filled with darkness, pain and misery.

Only Jesus Christ, the Great Deliverer, can cut your bondages and move you from Satan's kingdom of darkness into God's kingdom of light. He proved how very much He desires to do just that by shedding His blood in loving sacrifice for you. He paid the price of buying you back because He loves you infinitely more than you could ever imagine.

If you have not already done so, I urge you now to get down on your knees and accept that sacrifice and be washed in that blood. Tell the blessed Savior that you are willing to turn away from sin and ask Him to fill you with His Holy Spirit and present you to the Father as one of His very own. He and the Father will then come and live within you as they have promised, in a very intimate way.

This is the reason you were born, your glorious destiny — to become the dwelling place, the tabernacle of God forever and ever and ever.

The Good Shepherd is waiting, with outstretched arms.

"Come!"

Epilogue

*Therefore, behold, I will allure her, bring
her into the wilderness, and speak kindly
to her.*
*Then I will give her her vineyards from there,
And the valley of Achor [trouble] as a
door of hope.*
*And she will sing there as in the days of
her youth,
As in the day when she came up from the land
of Egypt.*
*And it will come about that in that day,
declares the Lord,
That you will call Me Ishi [my Husband] and
will no longer call Me Baali [my Master].*
*For I will remove the names of Baals [false
gods] from her mouth,
So that they will be mentioned by their
names no more.*
*In that day I will also make a covenant for
them with the beasts of the field,*

The birds of the sky,
And the creeping things of the ground.
And I will abolish the bow, the sword, and
war from the land,
And will make them lie down in safety.
And I will betroth you to Me forever;
Yes, I will betroth you to Me in
righteousness and in justice,
In lovingkindness and compassion,
And I will betroth you to Me in
faithfulness.
Then you will know the Lord.
(Hosea 2:14-20)

[Explanations in brackets are derived from the Hebrew.]

"Do you regret that you gave ten of the best years of your life to a system that failed you?" an ex-nun once asked me. After a moment's reflection, I responded, "No. Even though the system itself may have let me down, I spent those years searching for God and I think it must be written in a Book somewhere."

The painful experiences of my early life may have caused a huge vacuum within my soul, but the exceedingly good news is it required an immense God to fill it. I have no regrets. *"And we know that God causes all things to work together for good to those who love God, to those who are called according to His purpose"* (Rom. 8:28).

The religious life was, after all, one which I freely chose and at no time was I held against my will. In retrospect, I now realize that my own dysfunctional personality often impaired my relationships with other women, especially those in positions of authority.

The nuns with whom I shared those years were, for the most part, women of uncommon commitment and courage. I bear no animosity toward any of them; they did the best they could with what they had. With only human strength to attain superhuman ideals, it is understandable that most of our efforts resulted in frustration and failure. I wish I could share with those sisters the abiding peace and joy with which I have been blessed.

The romance that was initiated years ago continues to this day. I fell crazy-in-love with Jesus Christ because He first loved me. I've been held captive ever since.

Like all love stories, it has had its mountains and valleys, deserts and verdant fields. I have come perilously close to going over precipices, but my faithful Shepherd has always been there to rescue me. A few times I've gotten caught in the bramble bushes and with infinite tenderness, those nail-scarred hands have broken back the thorned branches and lovingly retrieved me. Sometimes I sense that He must shake His head and sigh, "Indeed, you are woolly-brained."

I used to become very discouraged about my lack of spiritual progress until I began to understand that salvation is a process, a pilgrimage. Although the initial justification is indeed the free, totally unmerited gift of God (John 3:16), our "moving on" from believer, to disciple, to overcomer requires the cooperation of our will with His grace. Basically, we just keep saying, "Yes, Lord, I will," and obeying Him and He does the work in us.

The difference between what I have just described and what I attempted to accomplish as a nun is explained very well in the following passage from page seven of a booklet entitled, *Entering Through the Gates*, by Dr. Robert Thompson.*

> God's grace comprises the blood, the Word, and the Holy Spirit. If it were not for the Holy Spirit, obedience to the written Word would be an exercise in asceticism. We are commanded to lay aside our whole Adamic nature with its lust, idolatry, malice, drunkenness, and witchcraft, and to put on the new man of love, joy and peace.
>
> Without the Holy Spirit, such a crucifixion, accompanied by the effort to be perfectly virtuous, would require a self-control that few human beings possess. It would be a nightmare of attempting to grind away every shred of carnal desire and to think, speak, and act virtuously.
>
> But God has given us His own Spirit, the Spirit of wisdom, power, love, joy, peace, understanding, and comfort. The Holy Spirit guides and strengthens us in every aspect of crucifixion and resurrection.
>
> What would be an impossible effort in self-improvement becomes a romance, a

---

* Trumpet Ministries, Inc; P.O. Box 1522; Escondido, CA 92033; reprinted by permission

joy, a song, a never-ending adventure leading to the city of glory....

Our heavenly Father is creating a Bride for His Son,
conformed to His divine image. As Eve once came out
of the side of the first Adam, this Wife, the true Church,
is being made into His likeness so that she will one day
enter into the pierced and glorified side of the New
Adam and become the eternal companion of the Lamb
of God. (See Eph. 5:25 and Rev. 21:2,9)

There is only one way in which we can become bone
of His bone and flesh of His flesh — by following in His
footsteps.

That blessed hope should fill each of our earthly moments with joy and loving expectation.

Keep following Jesus, and *don't give up*. We're going
to make it!

"Who is this coming up from the wilderness,
leaning on her beloved."
(Song of Solomon 8:5)